Advance Praise

"Practical advice from page[...]ries or lengthy case studies to extract key take-aways for working with and leading others. *We Can't Do It Alone* makes it easy to sharpen your skills now."

- **STACIE HAGAN** – SVP and Chief People Officer, Secureworks

"We Can't Do It Alone is an invaluable resource for any leader of any team who has to influence a diverse set of key partners, constituents, and stakeholders."

- **KEITH BRUCE** – President, Formula 1 Experiences; Former CEO and President of Super Bowl 50

"We Can't Do It Alone is filled with intuitive advice and ideas. I squirmed at times realizing how much improvement I can personally make."

- **ALICIA PHILIPP** – President, The Community Foundation for Greater Atlanta

"I absolutely love this book, not just as a business read but as one applicable for our personal lives as well."

- **SARAH BRYANT** – Senior Vice President of Finance, Comcast

Advance Praise for *We Can't Do It Alone*

"*We Can't Do It Alone* is a perfect primer on how to collaborate with and lead others with an underlying emphasis on values critical to a healthy workplace. Use it as a reference book to review regularly for reminders on best practices that work!"

- **KAREN E. KREIDER** – Consultant and Previous Chief Information Officer at NAPA Auto Parts, Ingram Micro, and Winn-Dixie

"*We Can't Do It Alone* elegantly outlines strategies and tactics we can all use to work better with others. I plan to re-read the first chapter every year it is so good!"

- **HENRY "HAWK" MCINTOSH** – The McIntosh Method

"*We Can't Do It Alone* elegantly summarizes the building blocks to work better with others and recognize and nurture critical relationships to achieve our personal and professional goals."

- **PAIGE LILLARD** – CEO, Beacon Consulting PBL, former Lead Judge for the Malcomb Baldridge Award for Performance Excellence, and VP, Global Business Transformation, Turner Broadcasting System, author of *LEAD, Getting from Hourly to Executive*

We Can't Do It Alone
BUILDING INFLUENCE
WITH SIMPLE STRATEGIES

Fred Jewell

FOREWORD BY JASON MOLFETAS

ENGAGED
WORLD
PRESS

Best wishes,
Fred Jewell

ISBN: 978-0-9996404-0-1

Cover Design by Joe Furmanek

ENGAGED
WORLD
PRESS

Published by
Engaged World Press, LLC
www.engagedworldpress.com

For Julie, Maddie and Max. Thanks for the inspiring dinner table conversations. I love you all more than you know.

For Dad. Thanks for your encouragement, wisdom and love.

And for my mom, Kate. We will have some catching up to do.

Contents

Foreword

As a frequent reader of leadership books, I can't help but notice that most of the insights contained in each book aren't really all that new. But that hasn't kept thousands of authors from trying their hand at a new way of looking at leadership and human behavior. The best books remind me about the things I know I should be doing every day to be more effective as a leader. We Can't Do It Alone does just that, and it does it very succinctly.

This engaging little book boils down the basics of getting things done through other people. Fred Jewell avoids expounding on elaborate theory and gets right down to the practical tactics we can all use to be more effective every day. And not just at work. In fact, perhaps the best thing about this book is that these simple ideas can be applied in all aspects of our lives, from dealing everyone we work with, to people in the community, and especially to our family - spouses, kids and even our own parents.

As a leader who has worked in the C-suite of several large companies, I recognize that leadership is all about influence, about getting things done through other people. And to get things done through other people, you need to make sure that those people also have the skills they need to influence and get things done through others. I highly recommend that everyone reading this book think through who they know who needs to read this book. If you're like me, you'll realize how much more productive we would all be if everyone we interacted with knew about the ideas outlined in this book and how to apply them every day.

Once you've read the book, I predict you'll want to keep it handy as a reference, something to give you that last minute idea before a challenging conversation or big meeting. I do. In the meantime, you'll enjoy the clarity and engaging anecdotes Fred Jewell provides in *We Can't Do It Alone*. I promise you'll benefit time and time again from the book, and I predict that you'll want to share it with the people around you. I have.

Jason D. Molfetas
Executive Vice President and Chief Marketing, Digital, and Business Development Officer
Amtrak Corporation

Introduction

"We Can't Do It Alone" started with a frustrated team trying to solve a difficult problem: how to get 2,000 people set in their ways to change the way they work. Our task was to improve the processes and the culture of a large Information Technology (IT) organization on a tough timeline. Our success or failure would be measured against an industry standard by third-party assessors. Because of contractual commitments tied to the achievement of these goals, millions of dollars were at stake.

I was assigned to lead the team that would drive the necessary changes through the organization. Part of my team consisted of five individuals, each one assigned to change a department of 150-500 technology professionals within the larger organization. Each of them had been working hard to make improvements, but they were all struggling to make progress. Frustrated and burned out, they said that without the authority to make people follow processes and behave in new ways, they alone were powerless to make any changes. After all, they were only one person trying to change the daily habits of as many as 500 people. I needed to find a way to amplify what each of them could do, to help them see that going it alone wasn't going to work.

I walked the team through a series of questions to help them think through what it would to take to get the authority they wanted. After talking it through with each other, they came to recognize that they would never get the authority to *make* people do anything. In fact, even if they did get the ultimate authority, the ability to hire-and-fire the people in the organization, they couldn't make anyone do anything they didn't want to do. Technology talent was (and still is) in very short supply. Our IT professionals could always quit whenever they wanted, and they'd probably get a new job right away. We needed to develop the influence skills it would take to get the rest of the organization on board with our contractual commitments.

I have always been fascinated with leadership and influence, why some people can get us to do things we wouldn't otherwise do. I'm not talking about using fear and intimidation like a mob boss or a third-world dictator...that's cheating in my book (and this *is* my book). Truly powerful people bring you onboard to an agenda and a journey that you both want to achieve. They are respected for their ability to be both a good person *and* to influence other people to do the things that are in everyone's best interest. That's real power.

I gathered a short list of ideas and practices that could help the team move forward. I delved into the research on influence and change, and began to watch which tactics worked best. I observed my team in action, noted what worked (and didn't work), and paid close attention to the best leaders in our organization.

Our workforce was highly educated, technically proficient, and motivated to deliver great results. But the things I was adding to my list were not covered in the technical or business courses our workforce had studied. Neither were they taught in high school, or grammar school. They were rarely covered anywhere in our formal education, even in the leadership and management training programs offered at our firm, one of the best in the world at training professionals. If we learned them, we learned them from our parents, grandparents, coaches, and mentors. We learned how to build relationships, inspire action, get work done with others and lead from extracurricular activities and sports we participated in growing up. But even when we have learned how to do these things, we often forget to apply them when we need them.

Eventually, I had a solid list of simple strategies we could use to improve our influence within the organization. I presented the ideas I had gathered to my team. They found the content useful, and they started to apply it. The changes in behavior were subtle, but the results were significant. Relationships improved. Confidence increased. Processes improved, and our delivery metrics reflected it.

Over time I added new content and began presenting these strategies to other groups like volunteer organizations and began to see how they could be applied across so much of our lives. Parents who heard me speak noted how these ideas could be applied with their children and spouses, and even with their own aging parents. The success I saw and the feedback I received on the usefulness of these strategies inspired me to continue to build the list and eventually to write this book.

One person acting alone can only do so much. One person marshalling the talent and passion of a group of people can move mountains. We can't do it alone. We need others rowing alongside us in the boat, and to get them in the boat with us, we need these simple strategies to build our influence and get them onboard.

If we keep these lessons of character, influence, and leadership front and center in our lives, we can make a bigger impact on the world. I often speak on this topic, and every time I do, I accidentally remind myself of the things I could do to amplify my own efforts. For you, I hope this book will be a useful tool in helping you to remember, and maybe even learn for the first time, these simple strategies for building influence. Because, whatever we want to achieve, we can't do it alone.

WE CAN'T DO IT ALONE

Climb the Influence Staircase

This book is about influence, about getting things done with and through other people. It's about moving people, teams, and organizations in the direction you want them to go.

You will find five main chapters, each applicable to a different part of the "Influence Staircase" shown below.

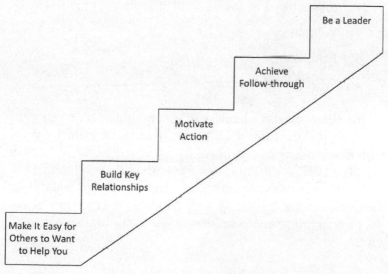

The Influence Staircase

Each chapter contains tactics that you can collect and put into your own personal toolkit. The book starts with laying the foundation and making it easy for others to want to help you, moves to building relationships, motivating action, and achieving follow-through. Once you've mastered these strategies, people are going to see you as a leader. The last chapter offers some additional strategies for maintaining your reputation for leadership over the long haul.

These simple strategies are applicable at work, in the community, and even at home. In each of those realms, we need skills that will help us influence:

- Bosses

- Team members

- Peers

- Clients and customers

- Partners and vendors

- Regulators and government officials

- Volunteers

- Parents

- Spouses and children

An important disclaimer is in order. Influence, when used for good, is a great thing. Influence, when used against people, with unfair, ill, or selfish intent, is an all-too-common form of evil. The tactics and principles I describe here are intended to be used responsibly and with integrity. Use them when your desired outcome is aligned with the desired outcomes of the people you are trying to influence. Use them to do some good for the world.

Make It Easy for Others to Want to Help You

How will we get people to help us and to follow us if they don't see us as worthy of their trust? What are some of the fundamental character traits, behaviors, and skills we need to consistently demonstrate that will put us in a position to influence others?

How people see us, our personal brand, is important. People talk, and there is a good chance they will be talking about us, especially if we are going to be in any kind of a position of leadership, power, or influence. Our reputation precedes us at work and in the community. With LinkedIn, Google, and Facebook, anyone can gather at least a few tidbits about us to form an impression prior to a first encounter.

This section of the book focuses on laying the groundwork for success. It's about the character traits, behaviors, and skills that will put us in a position to influence people. They are our ticket to the game.

Respect Everyone, All the Time

Starting off with something as simple as respect may seem trite, but we've all experienced people missing this key character trait. Respect is an example of a behavior subject to reciprocity. Reciprocity is that feeling that makes us want to give something back in return for something given to us. It is a universal value that almost all humans share (Cialdini, 1984). The idea of reciprocity gives rise to the phrase "mutual respect." It's a critical component in any relationship.

Be Polite

An old maxim says, "A drop of honey catches more flies than a gallon of gall." Being polite, in my usage here, means being respectful. For example, complimenting good behavior sticks with people and motivates in a positive way. Punishing bad behavior often results in toxic side effects and ends up de-motivating. It's always a good idea to keep the environment positive and constructive.

Being polite, especially in stressful situations, will help keep an argument or dispute from spinning out of control. Winston Churchill once signed a letter with, "I have the honor to be, Sir, with highest consideration, your obedient servant, Winston S. Churchill." (House of Commons, 1941) The letter was sent on December 8, 1941, to the Japanese Ambassador informing him that Britain was declaring war on his country. Churchill said about his closing, "Some people didn't like the ceremonious style, but after all, when you have to kill a man, it costs nothing to be polite." (Churchill, 1959)

Watch Your Mouth

"If you don't have something nice to say, don't say anything at all."
– Kate Jewell (my mom)

My mother was chock full of good advice. She taught us to avoid talking badly about other people when they're not present to defend themselves. There is an old saying that sums this up well. Before we speak about anyone else, put the words through this filter: "Is it true? Is it kind? Is it necessary?" We need to be able to answer "yes" to all three questions before we can be assured that the critique we are about to give someone, or the story we are about to tell about someone, is worth mentioning.

Gossip can be a good thing. In fact, research shows that gossip plays an important part in regulating a community. When people know that others will be talking about their bad behavior, they tend to behave better. But when we criticize our friend (or co-worker) Steve in front of our friend Dee when Steve isn't there, Dee is going to wonder what we say about Dee when she's not there.

Adopt the Platinum Rule

The Golden Rule says, "treat others the way you'd like to be treated." I've always thought that was a little short-sighted. The Platinum Rule, on the other hand, says, "treat others the way THEY want to be treated."

For example, my wife and I aren't the most sentimental people when it comes to celebrating holidays, our birthdays, or even our wedding anniversary. If one of our kids has a game on our anniversary, we'll gladly have dinner some other night, or maybe even skip it altogether. Early on in our marriage, my wife and I made Mother's Day plans that didn't involve my mother-in-law. Because we had more than one stop to make on Mother's Day, our thinking was that we'd be able to spend more time with her if we just got together with her the following Saturday. It was, after all, only six days later. My mother-in-law was really upset by this, and we were caught off guard. She wanted us to celebrate Mother's Day together, not a different day. We violated the Platinum Rule: treat others the way *they* want to be treated. We were treating her the way *we* would want to be treated. We don't miss Mother's Day with my wife's mom anymore.

Avoid Arguments

Dale Carnegie pointed out that we can never win an argument. We may win the point, but we've made someone else who might be an ally a loser, and nobody likes to be a loser (Carnegie, 1936). Better to ask cordial but challenging questions and see if we can influence a change in thinking.

As George Carlin said, "Never argue with an idiot. If you do, they will only bring you down to their level and beat you with experience." Take the high road and walk away from an argument that's not worth having.

Manage Your Passion

Passion is a great thing. Without passion, the great works of Martin Luther King, Mahatma Gandhi, and countless other leaders could never have happened. Passionate people are often inspiring, interesting, and entertaining. They are also usually very believable. But we can over-do it with passion.

If we over-do passion, we can come off as single-minded and inflexible. Politicians sometimes fall into this trap. Passionate politicians who run on a single-issue platform are no doubt passionate about their cause, but what about everything else? Their passionate focus on a narrow issue can create uncertainty, and people are not as likely to follow them.

Remember to balance your passion with the level of passion of your audience. Firing up your allies requires a high level of passion, but a more tempered and pragmatic approach is more successful when you are working with opponents and skeptics.

Stay Calm - Be Careful with Anger

Maintain your composure. Don't blow up, overreact, or otherwise go off the deep end. When we do lose control, people will wonder if we can control ourselves. Self-control is a characteristic we want to see in our leaders. People want to be influenced by and follow people they see as stable and in control.

Good leaders are aware of their emotions and harness them to their advantage. Leaders who rely on anger, intimidation, and force to get their way instill fear in their constituency (think mob boss or dictator). They push people in the direction they want them to go, rather than creating a pull by inspiring them with the possibilities.

Aristotle wrote, "Anyone can become angry. That is easy. But being angry with the right person, to the right degree, at the right time; that is not easy." Anger can be very powerful when we use it in small doses at the right time. People who are measured and laid back can get an extra kick out of anger when it's appropriate. My family, for instance, doesn't see me get angry very often, but when I do, they know that whatever motivated the anger is very important to me.

People prone to frequent anger are often dismissed with eye rolls or a "here we go again" reaction from the receiver of their anger. To remain credible, it pays to step back, calm down, and choose our words wisely.

Vent PRIVATELY

Some people just need to vent. They benefit from talking out their anger and frustration. When that venting targets the person whose actions provoked their anger or frustration, it can escalate to an argument and damage their relationship. Even if we choose to vent about others to a trusted friend, doing it too much can get tedious, even for a good friend. If you're someone who needs this kind of outlet, try venting on paper, or on your computer.

Upon Abraham Lincoln's death, in the drawers of his desk at the White House, his staff found scathing letters to his generals that conveyed his frustration with the lack of progress of the Union Army. He would write the letters, but he wouldn't mail them. Lincoln knew that they would not have the desired effect, but the letters helped him "get it all out" and then mull it over a while to become more objective.

Unfortunately, in today's instant communication world, it's easy to post our frustrations to a large audience very quickly: think flaming emails, angry Facebook posts, or whiny tweets. If you need to vent, go ahead and vent. Just don't post it or send it until you've taken some time to calm down. Just walk away. Do whatever works for you to settle down. Sleep on it. Take the time to get out from under that emotional state, then come back and read what you've written. You'll probably find that the extra time you took to calm down results in a communication that is more objective, focused, and effective...and much less emotional.

Managing emotion can be a challenge, but having the ability to step outside of our heads to assess our emotional state is a critical influence skill. To help you observe yourself from the outside, try asking yourself these questions: Is your current state helping you be more effective with others, or is it hurting you? Are the people you are trying to influence going to react the way you want to the emotions you're displaying? The ability to recognize and control our emotions, along with understanding our audience, are both keys to helping us build influence so we don't have to go it alone.

Be Clear

Communication skills, both written and spoken, are foundational for anyone with influence. Being clear allows those who can help us to know exactly how they can help. Plenty of books have been written on communications skills, but I have found the simple tactics in this table to be effective ways to improve our writing and speaking skills.

	Bad	Better
1	We will utilize the process.	We will use the process.
2	Thank you for your cooperation in this matter.	Thanks for your help.
3	The plan is created by the project manager.	The project manager creates the plan.
4	Don't forget your umbrella.	Remember to take your umbrella.

#1 - Use Simpler Words

Could you use simple words instead of complex ones? For example, one of my pet peeves in business writing is the overuse of the word "utilize." Utilize means the same thing as "use," but it has three syllables compared to one, and seven letters compared to three. Using words like utilize can make it look like you're trying to appear smart. You are smart, so use simple words.

#2 - Be Conversational

I have noticed that junior people in an organization often write more formally than they speak, especially when they are writing to people more senior to them in the organization. For some reason, they think that the higher you get in an organization, the more complex the writing and the language gets. Having worked with people at the top of many organizations, I can tell you that the opposite is true. Executives like clarity and simplicity in their communication, and keeping it simple and conversational is best. Be careful, however, to avoid being too informal, injecting what I'll call a "texting" style into your writing. An email to your boss reading, "Hey. Finished the report. Golf? YOLO" is crossing the line.

To come across more authentic and confident, try writing like you would speak to that person. For example, instead of ending an email with, "Thank you for your cooperation in this matter," try "Thanks for your help." Have you ever heard the phrase "thank you for your cooperation in this matter" come up in conversation? And to top it off, who wakes up in the morning looking forward to "cooperating"? But everyone wants to "help."

Be brief.

#3 - Use Active Voice

A great way to simplify our writing is to use active voice instead of passive voice. Active voice sentences have a clear subject, and the subject appears before the verb. Consider these three sentences:

1. The plan will be created.

2. The plan will be created by the project manager.

3. The project manager creates the plan.

The first sentence is passive voice, making it less clear. People describing a process often exclude the actor in a sentence by using passive voice, e.g., "The plan will be created." That's usually a cop-out, used when we don't know who actually *is* going to create the plan. If we publish our process with sentences like that, accountability for that given task goes undefined. If that happens often enough within an organization, nobody knows who is supposed to be doing what.

The second sentence is also passive voice. It conveys the same information as the third sentence, but the third sentence is written in active voice. The active voice sentence has fewer words and syllables. Using active voice can help turn that five-page document into four solid, clear pages instead.

#4 - FLIP the Negatives

To make your communication more positive, motivating, and brief, rephrase each sentence to eliminate the negative words such as "no," "not," and "never." Be sure to write and speak about what is rather than what is not. The change in the tone can be astounding, turning a downer of an email into something positive and focused on what will happen and what will be achieved.

This principle also has an important effect on how our brains process information. Consider the sentence:

"Don't forget to bring your umbrella to the game."

Eliminating "not" in that sentence makes it:

"Remember to bring your umbrella to the game."

First, we've eliminated a word from the sentence. Second, we are planting the idea of what we want the person to do rather than the thing we do not want them to do. We help their brain picture success rather than failure. When we think "remember to bring the umbrella," we envision ourselves picking it up and carrying it. When we think about "forgetting the umbrella," we think about the soaking feeling we'll have in the downpour. It pays to picture the words that describe a successful outcome.

Our readers will see us as authentic, clear, practical, and positive if we apply these four simple principles to our writing. It does take work. Blaise Pascal once said, "I have only made this letter long because I have not had time to make it shorter." Editing takes work. Make the effort.

Be Positive

"We'll get it done, we always do" is one of my mottos. It's a refreshing thought when things are overwhelming and not going so well.

A positive attitude is attractive. People enjoy being around others who inspire them, who point out the good that is happening, who radiate positive energy. Positive people appear more confident and, therefore, more likely to deliver.

In his book *Hard Optimism*, Price Pritchett points out research that shows optimism and pessimism are not opposite ends of the same spectrum, but rather lie on independent axes. This means someone can be both highly optimistic and highly pessimistic.

This chart illustrates this concept.

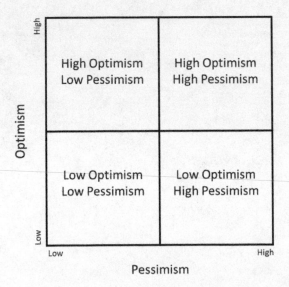

- High optimism/high pessimism people may be outwardly positive while second guessing decisions and worrying about failing.

- High optimism/low pessimism people may be enthusiastic about new ideas while being prone to taking unnecessary risks.

- Low optimism/high pessimism people can seem cynical but may also be very good at identifying risk.

- Low optimism and low pessimism people are skeptical, not overly positive about the likelihood of success, but not negative, either. They just plow through.

So being optimistic doesn't mean you can't be pessimistic, too.

Being optimistic also turns out to be good for our health. In a 50-year study of a group of nuns living in a convent, the nuns who tested as highly optimistic tended to outlive their more negative sisters by an average of 10 years. This was a pretty amazing finding, especially when you consider that if you don't smoke, it only buys you seven years (Pritchett, 2007). So, whatever you do, don't be a grumpy smoker.

To be more optimistic, consider the words that you use most often. When my kids were about 12 and 9, I was concerned about some language that was creeping into our dinner conversations, complaining words like hate, disgusting, annoying, gross, stupid, and dumb. I decided to set up a contest to see if I could stamp out this bad behavior. Any time we said these words, we put a tick mark next to the offender's name on a score sheet hanging in the kitchen. The actual score sheet is shown here, ketchup stain and all. Each tick mark was worth a dime. Whoever had the fewest tick marks at the end of the month received the cash represented by everyone else's tick marks.

ANTI-WORD LIST

HATE

DISGUSTING

ANNOYING

GROSS

STUPID

DUMB

DAD ~~IIII~~ ~~IIII~~ IIIII / 3.30

MOM ~~IIII~~ ~~IIII~~ ~~IIII~~ ~~IIII~~ IIIII IIII / 4.40

MADDIE ~~IIII~~ III / 704

MAX ~~IIII~~ ~~IIII~~ ~~IIII~~ ~~IIII~~ ~~IIII~~ IIIII ~~IIII~~ ~~IIII~~ III / 4.30

Our daughter, the most diligent listener of the bunch, was the best at busting everyone else. Our son, who really didn't care much but still didn't like being busted by his sister, came in third, edging out his mother who came in last. But clearly both Mom and Dad were having an influence on the tone of the conversation, not just the kids. After four weeks of the contest, it was amazing how much our conversation become less whiny, complaining, and gossipy. End result: it was much more pleasant at the dinner table, and the better, more positive language embedded itself in everything else we did.

Decide Well

Author Matthew Kelly said it best: When deciding on any specific course of action, choose the course that makes you the "best version of yourself." (Kelly, 1999)

We usually don't remember what someone decided to do about a given situation for very long. But we do remember how someone goes about deciding – it is a defining aspect of their character. Ethics and good judgement ensure that people are treated fairly. Transparency in how you came to your decision also helps people appreciate the nuances and challenges at play in your decisions.

Remember to decide based on data and fact, not on innuendo and vague statements. For example, someone might come to you with an issue where their colleagues are not completing their work on time and say something like, "They are always late." Step back to understand the problem more completely: Are they always late, or only sometimes? Why are they late? How late are they? What is the effect of being late? Try to understand the important facts before you decide, and then take action.

Go with Your Gut – It's Smarter than You Think

If the data and facts aren't enough to come to a clear, fact-based decision, go with your gut, literally. Researchers have determined that our gastroenterological system contains about half a billion neurons, which is about five times as many neurons as in our spinal cord. Our gut secretes about half of the dopamine in our system, which is associated with pleasure and motivation, and about 90% of our serotonin, the neurotransmitter that helps regulate mood and behavior.

While scientists are just beginning to scratch the surface on the importance of the gut in the function of our brain and overall nervous system, it's likely that the feelings that come from "gut instinct" when struggling with a decision are providing real information. Take gut feeling into account and learn to trust it.

Take the Initiative

People sometimes avoid taking initiative. If there's a problem, we assume someone else will take care of it. We might see something that needs to be improved, but don't bother to start because someone "in charge" hasn't asked us to do it. We're comfortable doing what we're doing, and doing something different would push us out of our comfort zone and put us at risk. It doesn't have to be that way. As many great leaders have asked over the centuries: "If not me, who? If not now, when?"

People avoid taking the initiative because they're too busy, distracted, lazy, or afraid of failure. Being busy is understandable, but being afraid of failure is something that we should all work to overcome. IBM's founder, TJ Watson said, "The way to succeed is to double your failure rate." If you're not failing occasionally, you're probably not pushing yourself hard enough.

How about volunteering to be the person who creates the first draft of the report or presentation? The vast majority of what you create will survive, while only a small percentage will be changed or edited by others. Think about all that influence you will have when you set the tone and frame future discussion.

When people are gathering in a conference room for a meeting and there are people you haven't met yet, try walking over to introduce yourself. You'll establish yourself as a leader and project an aura of confidence and initiative.

We've all seen people who complain about something but take no initiative to attempt to fix the problem or influence those who can. It's better to step outside of our comfort zones and take the initiative to change the things that bother us. Don't be a victim. Remember, we are free to choose who we want to be, who we want to be with, where we want to live, what we want to do. If we're not happy, we can do something about it.

People like to be around other people who make things happen. Making things happen requires initiative. Take it.

Be Persistent

People are busy, and often overwhelmed, especially leaders within the organization. Most of the time, when leaders don't respond to our initial request to meet, talk, or review something, it's not because they don't like us, or they're not interested in our project; they're just busy.

Persistence pays off. My own experience has been that it often takes at least three attempts to get through the noise in a person's inbox. After that, the success rate starts to trickle off, but I've tried as many as five times and finally received a "Thank you for being persistent. My calendar and inbox are out of control. I would love to speak with you about..."

When you are being persistent, it pays to try to get someone's attention through multiple channels. I find that too many people rely solely on email, even when the people they want to connect with sit only 20 feet away. Get up and talk to them in person. Walk with them in the hallway. Call them on their office line and leave a voice message. Using multiple channels is smart, but unless it's a true emergency, it's best to avoid using all of them at the same time lest you create an annoying and unnecessary sense of urgency.

Be careful with texts or calls on personal mobile phones. Those channels can be very personal depending on who you are dealing with, so make sure you know how that person feels about mobile phone calls or texts before you use that channel. Persistence indicates passion. As your persistence increases on any given issue, people will correlate that to the importance of the issue to you. When something is important to you, demonstrate that with persistence. Martin Luther King, one of history's great influencers, didn't change the world with one speech or one demonstration. It took years of persistent effort and recruiting millions of other people to make change happen. Be persistent, and eventually, the people you are trying to influence will come around.

Questions for Reflection: Make It Easy for Others to Want to Help You

Key ideas and questions to consider:

Respect everyone, all the time.

1. Who might you be taking for granted? How might you find ways to be more gracious and polite?

2. Do you always consider whether something is true, kind, and necessary before you say it?

3. Think of a situation where you applied the Golden Rule. How could it have turned out differently if you had applied the Platinum Rule?

Manage your passion.

4. How might you recognize when you are getting too passionate about a point or an idea? What can you do to calm yourself down?

5. Are you someone who uses passion and anger productively, or do passion and anger often prevent you from meeting your goals or accomplishing a task? Would a close confidant agree with you?

6. Do you ever publicly vent or whine about things online? How could you change what you write in social media and email to create a more positive personal brand?

Be clear.

7. Do you sometimes use big words on purpose, or resort to jargon? Which of the rules outlined in this section could you adopt to make your writing and speaking clearer?

8. How could you use peer pressure to encourage everyone at work to use simpler words, shorter sentences, active voice, and eliminate negative words?

Be positive.

9. Could you make a more conscious effort to look at situations from a more positive and optimistic viewpoint? If so, how?

10. Do you ever hang out with a group of people who are mostly negative? What could you do to encourage less cynicism?

Decide well.

11. How could you improve your decision-making process? Are you probing where you should and gathering as many facts as you can?

12. Do you trust your gut? Do you think you should?

Take the initiative.

13. How could you take more initiative at work, at home, or in the community? What is holding you back?

Be persistent.

14. Could you be more persistent? Do you give up too quickly when someone doesn't respond to a call or an email? Do you keep trying, three, four, or even five times?

Build Key Relationships

Once we've established ourselves as someone others want to help, we can focus on building relationships. As a species, we have a fundamental need to be connected to other people. Relationships are good for us. We're wired for them. Having at least a few deep relationships is one of the proven keys to happiness (Haidt, 2006). The people with whom we have good relationships want to help us and we want to help them.

This section could be subtitled, "How to get people to like us." People want to help the people they like. The strong influence principle of reciprocity is also at work here. We tend to like people who like us. We do nice things for people who do nice things for us.

We like it when we feel important, and we feel bad when we are ignored, marginalized, or disenfranchised. The tactics in this chapter help us help other people feel important. And other people *are* important. If they weren't, why would we want to build a relationship with them?

Of course, as I've mentioned earlier in the book, it is critical to apply these ideas with caring intent towards the people you are building a relationship with. Be genuine and honest with the intent of helping others.

Manage First Impressions

First impressions matter. They matter a lot. The good news is that we can usually control the way we make a first impression.

Our brains are very efficient at making quick decisions about whether someone is a threat or an ally, someone we want to be associated with, or someone to be avoided. We make snap judgments about someone's competency, trustworthiness, passiveness or aggressiveness, and we do this in as little as 1/10 of a second the very first time we meet. (Todorov, 2006).

Once people have a first impression, it's hard to change it. In fact, we filter the information we receive after a first impression to reinforce our first impression (Todorov, 2006). Changing the first impression we have made on someone is usually an arduous task.

Before we can even start to worry about first impressions, it's important to step back and think about who we need to meet. This is a critical step most people forget. List all the people you should be meeting with on a regular basis to be effective in your role, note why you need to know them, develop a strategy for getting to know them, and then maintain that relationship.

To get the ball rolling in the right direction with the people you need to work with, do everything you can to make a good first impression. That means being deliberate about how you approach the encounter. One of the keys to a good first encounter is to consider the mood or current frame of mind of the person we're trying to meet.

How well you are perceived and remembered in an initial encounter is based as much on the other person's feelings at the time as it is on what you do. Our brains are wired to store feelings associated with an encounter much more easily than the data and facts about situation. I bet you remember a lot about how you felt when you had your first kiss. Songs often bring back very specific feelings and memories. We are emotional people, and we associate things and people with feelings about events we've shared. The person with whom we will have a first encounter will be in some emotional state when we meet them. For example, they might be relaxed, happy, joyous, or perhaps stressed, scattered, angry, or sad. If we were feeling sad the first time we met someone, we will subconsciously associate that person with that sad emotion. So, we must be aware of the emotional state of the person we are meeting for the first time.

The context for a first impression is often controllable. Let's say that you lead a team that provides travel and transportation support to a key executive in your company. You and your team may be very, very good, but inevitably something will go wrong with a flight or a hotel reservation and you'll end up in a meeting with the executive you support so they can tell you about their bad experience. Do you really want to have that meeting be the first time that you meet that executive?

Instead, what if you take the time to introduce yourself to that executive when things are running smoothly, perhaps at a team celebration, a holiday party, or some other event where the executive will be relaxed and receptive? That first introduction while they are in a good mood will associate you with that positive mood, rather than the stress of a crisis. It is important to build up the emotional capital that you get from a pleasant introduction before having to deal with a stressful or contentious situation.

Before we meet someone, we should think about the context surrounding the other person. How do they feel? What's going on with them at this moment? Are they in a hurry, or relaxed?

Get to know people when they're relaxed and happy. If you can't control the timing of your introduction, then make sure you nail the physical aspects of a great introduction. Here they are.

Say and Do the Right Things

In the United States, when you meet someone new, remembering to do these things will go a long way towards a good first impression:

1. Smile.

2. Look the person you are meeting in the eye (long enough to notice their eye color).

3. Say your name clearly and confidently.

4. Deliver a firm handshake. A good, American business handshake is the same for a man and for a woman. A firm palm-to-palm handshake is always appropriate.

5. Listen for their name. If you don't understand it or don't think you heard it correctly, have the confidence to say, "I'm sorry, I didn't quite hear that. What is your name again?" Use their name in the conversation to show them that you listened, to make the conversation feel more personal, and to help you remember it in the future.

6. From there on out in the conversation, listen, and focus your ENTIRE attention on the conversation, on that individual. Keep your focus on their eyes. Avoid looking around the room. When you feel the need to look away, look at something innocuous, like your glass, your shoes, or a painting. Try hard not to be distracted by other people, TV screens, or your phone. That other person needs to be the most important thing in the world to you at that moment. They will know if they're not. Truly listen to what they are saying.

7. Work hard to keep the conversation positive and focused on non-controversial topics. Avoid being

critical or negative in initial conversations. Project optimism and happiness.

It's important to note here that proper and effective introductions are highly dependent upon culture. When you travel, take the time to understand the expectations and customs of the local culture.

Basic ideas, right? Yet it's remarkable how many people don't do them. Work at them, forever.

Listen with Everything You Have

Listening is key to leadership and influence. Listening creates understanding and connection.

Listen with your ears. Listen with your eyes. Listen with your gut. Think about what you've just heard and observed. Often, when we're talking with someone else, we don't listen with our ears very well. That's because we're not totally present, not "in the moment." We're too busy thinking about what we're going to say next, and what the other person thinks about us.

When I speak on this topic, I ask the people in the room whether they are bad at remembering names. Usually most people in the room raise their hand. I then challenge the audience to fix that, to never answer yes to that question again. You may have assumed that people who are good with names have a natural ability to remember names. But ask why they are so good with names and most of them will tell you that they had to work at it. Most of us aren't naturals. If you're ready to make the effort, try these steps:

1. Recognize when you're about to walk into a conversation, or a party, when you're going to have to remember names. Prepare yourself to listen and focus on getting everyone's names right from the start.

2. When you do get to hear her name, listen.

3. Repeat back to her, "Nice to meet you, Jennifer."

4. Use her name in the subsequent conversation: "So, Jennifer, how long have you..."

5. Use it when ending the conversation: "Jennifer, it was a pleasure to meet you."

6. When you're walking away from the conversation, repeat her name in your head and two key facts you learned about her.

7. Try to associate her name with someone famous, say Jennifer Lopez, or something about their hobbies that is alliterative and easy to remember, like Jazzy Jennifer. Visualize her playing a piano. The possibilities with rhyming, animals, cartoons, or superheroes are endless. The more off-the-wall the image you create, the easier it will be to remember.

8. When you get back to having some alone time with your phone, enter them into your contacts list. In the notes section, write down the quick facts you remember, and context in which you met, e.g., "Jennifer Smith, jazz pianist, met at Ashish's party, originally from Charlotte." If you don't have a phone handy, jot it down when you get to a pen and paper, or write the facts and the context on the back of their business card for later entry into the software tool (or little black book) you use to store your contacts. One colleague, a consultant and coach, told me how, when she was a student working in the VIP lounge of a major hotel chain, she would duck into the kitchen and pull out a small notepad she carried with her at work to jot down the names of the VIP guests she had just met so she could always refer to them by name. Eventually, she got good enough at memorizing names right away that she didn't need to use the notepad anymore. She had rewired her brain to be good at remembering names. And so can we.

Salespeople write down what they learned about their prospects all the time. Why? Because remembering important things about a prospect makes them feel important, and it helps build rapport. It's a business best practice, and it applies personally, too. Your friends, co-workers, acquaintances, and service providers are important, just like your customers. It's a good idea to treat them that way.

Work hard to remember names. Names are important. Dale Carnegie said, "A person's name is to that person, the sweetest, most important sound in any language." (Carnegie, 1936) People notice when you don't remember their name, but more importantly, they notice when you do, because it shows you care about them.

Watch Your Body Language

Awareness of body language is a key skill for someone with influence. By paying attention to body language, we can get a sense of whether someone is bored, frustrated, defensive, passionate, or engaged.

But what about your own body language? What signals are you sending when you're listening to someone else? Our body language usually gives away how engaged we are in a conversation, how well we are listening, and ultimately, how much we care about the other person.

Behaviors to avoid include:

- Crossing your arms. It closes us off, making us look nervous and defensive, like we have something to hide.

- Telegraphing our "tells." Almost everyone has a tell. A friend of mine said her staff pointed out that she would pull her hair back behind her ear before she would "go in for the kill" with a cutting question or statement. A common tell for others is to pick up a cup of coffee or water when they are nervous about something that has just been said in a meeting. Be aware of the unconscious movements and postures that convey your emotion.

- Looking at things that are distracting, or that the other person thinks might be distracting, like your phone, a television screen, or other people in the room.

- Looking at the clock or your watch. Unless you want to send a clear signal that you want to move on and/or want the conversation to end, don't do it.

Knowing your body language tendencies will help others experience you as a much better listener.

Play Talk Show Host

One of the easiest ways to build a relationship is to find something we have in common with the other person. To do this, picture yourself as a great talk show host asking great questions that the person you are speaking with will find interesting.

The key is to focus on things they will find interesting to get them talking about things they like to talk about. Once you get them talking, you'll find things you have in common. Researchers have shown that the result is chemical. Upon discovering something in common with someone else, our brain releases a dose of oxytocin, the neurochemical associated with connection (Rock, 2009, p. 166).

By asking questions, we demonstrate interest, which indicates that we like the other person. Reciprocity, as mentioned earlier in the section titled "Respect Everyone, All the Time," kicks in here, too: We tend to like people who like us.

The more questions we ask, the more we listen, the more connections we find. The more we talk about those things we have in common, the more closeness we feel to the other person. During the conversation, it's also important to demonstrate empathy when you feel it. "I can imagine how you feel. The same thing happened to me."

If you find yourself struggling to get past small talk in a conversation, try this: when a person tells you a story, identify the key events in that story, drill down and ask details about the decisions they made during those events and the feelings they had. For instance, a conversation might go like this:

You: So, Lara, how long have you been in Atlanta?

Lara: We moved here five years ago. (Note: you've stumbled upon an event, the move.)

You: Where did you move from?

Lara: Chicago.

You: Why did you decide to move here?

Lara: I took a new position at XYZ Company.

You: How clear a decision was it to take that new job?

Lara: Well, the job was great. But convincing the family to move was more difficult. My husband was a professor at the local college, and my high school son and middle school daughter weren't very excited about the idea.

You: How are they doing now?" or "How did you handle that sales pitch?" Or "What type of professor is your husband?" Any one of those paths will expand the conversation.

Your starter question, how long have you been in Atlanta, followed by three more follow-up questions, has revealed where this person is from (you might be able to talk about that city, or maybe you're from there, too), where they work (you may have worked there, or know someone who does), that Lara has a family, that her husband is a professor, that she has a middle school daughter and a high school son. Those few questions hold lots of potential for a connection.

The paradoxical outcome of a great conversation where you ask a lot of questions is that people will begin to find you interesting, even if you do very little of the talking. It is important to contribute to the conversation by revealing details about yourself (see section titled "Open Up"), but people often find you fascinating if you simply ask good questions.

Ask a Favor

We usually think that doing favors for others will, well, win their favor. While that can be a good tactic (see the next section "Do Something Positively Unexpected"), doing the opposite can be a great way to build a relationship. In other words, try asking the person you want to build a relationship with for a favor. It's important to be sure that the favor is something that he will enjoy doing, and it has to be something that's easy for him to do.

Asking a favor, or asking for help of any kind, puts you in a subordinate position to the person who has what you want or need. This can be a minor, and sometimes a major, positive status bump for the person doing the favor or providing the help. The person doing the favor feels important, that they have something you don't.

Benjamin Franklin used to borrow books from people he was trying to build a relationship with. A book is easy to loan. By asking to borrow your book, Franklin was implying that he shared similar interests with you and wanted to know what you know (presuming you have read the book and internalized some of the wisdom contained within it). And it was obvious that you had something he didn't: the book itself. All those things would make you feel important, even if only a little bit. And Franklin, making you feel important, got you to like him a bit more.

Easy things to ask for include a recipe for a dish someone prepared, a decorator for a house you thought looked great, the store where they found a particular object, or a recommendation for a service provider. Remember, it has to be the right kind of favor, easy to give, not "would you help me move from my apartment into my new house" or "can I borrow your new car to go on a date?" Stick to the little stuff.

Do Something Positively Unexpected

Surprise someone by doing something that they wouldn't expect. Intention is everything here. You have to be genuine, without expecting something in return.

One simple, unexpected gesture could be sending a handwritten thank you or congratulations note. You might think that this doesn't fall into the category of unexpected, but it is. Few people take the time to buy personalized stationery and set aside the time to write a handwritten note. A colleague pointed out that receiving these notes can be so powerful and unexpected that we feel like we should write a thank you note for the sender's thank you note!

Be Openly Genuine

Be yourself and put yourself out there. Some of us are more naturally good at this than others, but almost everyone has room to improve. There are many ways to be authentic and genuine.

Offer a Compliment

When you see or hear something cool about someone else, acknowledge it. Congratulate him on an accomplishment, or compliment his performance, but only if you really mean it.

This can be a difficult thing for some people to do. Like asking for help, it puts you in a subordinate position to someone who achieved the accomplishment. However, when you genuinely respect what someone has done, and you mention it, it can be a very powerful relationship builder. To supercharge a compliment, put it in writing. A handwritten congratulations note can leave a powerful impression.

Laugh, Especially at Yourself

Be human. If you screw something up, don't try to cover it up. Laugh at it. Be honest and genuine. Nobody likes perfect people, and most people will forgive others who promptly admit a mistake and work to fix the problems they caused. In addition, being authentic and admitting our flaws can result in an instant connection when the person we are trying to influence can commiserate.

I once had a demanding client who was driving our consulting team hard. While I was away visiting other clients, my team reviewed a proposal with her. In the proposal, we had added some cost as contingency for some potential risks associated with the project. I was standing in a rental car bus to the airport, my arm wrapped around a pole, when I received a text that the proposal was accepted. Instead of waiting for a more appropriate time and place to try to compose a text, I thumbed back "Great job, team. I'm glad to hear Linda didn't choke on the amount for contingency." I meant to send that text to my team member who was leading the proposal, named Leslie. Instead, I sent it to the person next on my contact list, my client, Linda. I recognized the mistake immediately, and texted Linda, "Well...obviously that last text was not intended for you. I'm such a bonehead! I'm really looking forward to working with you on the project. Have a great weekend."

Then, I waited. By the time I was on the plane home, Linda had texted back "LOL. No worries. Have a great weekend." For the rest of the project, my new client (and my team) gave me crap about that mistake, but we all laughed about it, and often. It made me human, and it deepened our new relationship.

Self-deprecating humor can be very charming. Be sure to balance it with competence, or you can damage your credibility.

Open Up

I once coached someone who received feedback that she seemed too salesy, almost artificial. Thinking through the behaviors I was observing, I noticed that while she was genuine in her interest in others, funny, friendly, and great at remembering names and details about her customers, I also noticed that people knew very little about her. I coached her to open up and share more details and stories about herself and her family, even if those stories were embarrassing.

She considered the advice, and realized that she was a very private person and had not been sharing much with others. She took the advice to heart, and it had a dramatic effect on how she came across to others.

Relationship-building is a two-way street. It pays to open up a little bit. If you haven't shared something interesting or embarrassing, you probably won't get past that threshold of trust. Keep the conversation scales tipped in favor of others. Just remember to share things about yourself to build rapport.

Adapt Your Style

While it's important to be openly genuine, it's also important to adapt our style to fit in with the people we want to influence. When we want to fit in, we automatically start to adopt the posture, rate of speech, and gestures of the people we are trying to fit in with, and that's all (usually) done subconsciously.

Research has shown that people who are subtly mimicked are more likely to like their mimicker. Waitresses who adapt their style to the customers they serve get bigger tips (van Baaren, Holland, Steenaert, & van Knippenberg, Mimicry for money: Behavioral consequences of imitation, 2003, pp. 393-398). College students take only milliseconds to unconsciously start synchronizing their movements with their friends (Hatfield, Rapson, & Le, 2009).

Behaviors of people we hang around with, in general, are contagious. You are more likely to overeat with your friends who overeat. If your friends drink, you are more likely to drink. If your friends smoke, you are more likely to smoke. We naturally adapt to and mimic the people we're with.

Because this natural tendency is so strong, it's important to consciously adapt your style when you need to. For example, when I was a young consultant, I was one of the chief proponents of a "business casual" work environment. At that time, all men wore suits and ties, and the women wore business suits. I was all for khaki's and a nice shirt. I lobbied heavily for the policy change, and when it happened, I took full advantage of it.

When it came time for me to be considered for promotion to a senior executive position, one of my mentors pulled me aside and said, "If you want the promotion, you should dress the part." In our culture, senior executives in the firm wore nice dress slacks, shoes you could shine, and a sport coat, or they wore traditional business suits and ties. If I was going to fit in with this crowd, I needed to adapt. It was a small concession, but with the changes, I did look the part, I fit better into the culture at the executive level, and it helped me get the promotion.

I'm not advocating changing who you are to fit in, or making concessions that go against your values and morals. But small concessions in how we dress, the things we read, or the activities we participate in, can help us build a relationship with people who are important to us and help build our influence.

Be Available, be Familiar, be Nearby

Scientists call it propinquity. It's being close physically to something or someone else. This may seem incredibly obvious, but being near others is important to building strong relationships.

Close your eyes and think of a friend who is very different from you demographically, ethnically, and/or economically.

How did you get to know that person? It's likely you lived with them or near them in college, shared an office cubicle with them, or played together in a band or on a sports team. Strong relationships can result from simply being available and being familiar.

We also usually come to like things we are exposed to repeatedly. Parisians hated the Eiffel Tower when it was first built. They came to love it, over time, as it became more familiar (Heath & Heath, 2010, p. 254). Strangely, we even have a bias towards careers that sound like our own names: There are a disproportionate number of lawyers named Lawrence and dentists named Dennis and Denise (Pelham, Mirenberg, & Jones, 2002, pp. 469-87). We tend to like people whose names sound familiar. I married a girl named Julie. And her married name became Julie Jewell. You make the call.

This principle has significant implications for how we handle space at work. As the leader of a team that built software development processes and then deployed them to mostly less-than-receptive organizations, we leveraged this concept heavily. When we were developing the processes, we all sat together in the same place. This propinquity of process developers served us well to build a strong team and a strong process.

When it came time to get the rest of the organization to use the process, to our team's dismay, we made them move and sit close to the teams that they were teaching to use the process. This sometimes meant a move across town to a different location, and at a minimum meant a move to another part of our floor or a different floor in our high-rise. I passed along some wisdom from one of my mentors:

"You can't shoot a moose if you're sitting in the lodge."

It worked. It took some time, but the managers we had charged with rolling out the new processes built close relationships with the teams they were supporting.

When you're building something new, bring the people working on building that thing together in one place. When you're ready to get other people to use it, get your teams to move out and sit with the teams who need to use it. The relationships your team builds will make it much easier to influence the organization to adopt that new asset.

The "virtual" or telecommuting nature of the work done in many organizations makes propinquity almost impossible. But better use of the tools available to us can make a huge difference. Consider these tips for making people working remotely feel more "close" to one another:

- **Gather**: When forming a new virtual team, do everything you can to bring the team physically together to establish an initial relationship. As new people join, bring the team together again in person to get to know the new team members, and for the new person to get to know the team. This will build trust and help people recognize the body language and facial expressions that are associated with the comments on the other end of the line.

- **Greet**: At the beginning of the day, send a quick "good morning" chat message to your team members with a little banter about the happenings of the day.

- **Chat**: Encourage your team to dial in a few minutes early to conference calls to allow for some chit chat. Spend some time socializing and sharing stories.

- **Celebrate**: Plan virtual birthday parties, virtual happy hours and other virtual social happenings. A friend shared a story of a virtual celebration with two co-workers who she had worked with remotely for more than two years. "One was in Connecticut, one was in South Carolina and one in Southern California, but on the phone, at the same moment, we virtually clinked celebratory glasses. We all remember and refer to it occasionally." What a fun way to build a relationship.

These small ideas can go a long way to making a virtual work environment more engaging. But there is never a substitute for being physically near someone else to get to know them.

Deliver!

We establish competence and integrity by delivering what we promise to deliver, always. Delivering what we said we would deliver is especially important early in a relationship. Under-promise and over-deliver. By demonstrating we can be counted on, we set the foundation for a trusting relationship.

Questions for Reflection: Build Key Relationships

Key ideas and questions to consider:

Manage first impressions.

1. Who do you need to meet? What upcoming event might be a good opportunity to catch them in a good mood, on a good day?

Say and do the right things.

2. Are you always diligent about being truly present during an introduction to someone else or do you sometimes have thoughts racing through your head so you're not really listening? What could you do better in terms of eye contact, handshake, smiling, being engaged?

Listen with everything you have.

3. How well do you truly listen to another person in a conversation? What could you do better?

4. If you're the kind of person who says, "I'm bad with names," are you prepared to stop saying that and start making the extra effort it takes to be good at remembering names?

Play talk show host.

5. What are some great questions you ask to generate good conversations and insights into others? What are some other questions you could use to figure out what makes someone tick?

Ask a favor.

6. Think of someone with whom you'd like to deepen your relationship. What simple favor could you ask of them to make them feel good about helping you out?

Do something positively unexpected.

7. What could you do for someone else today that would make their day, or even "make their moment?"

Be openly genuine.

8. What could you do to be more authentic? Could you find ways to compliment others more often, or laugh at yourself to help everyone see that you're only human?

Adapt your style.

9. What small concessions could you make to better fit into the group of people you are trying to influence?

Be available, be familiar, be nearby.

10. Are you truly available to the people you want to influence? How can you adjust your schedule and work habits to be physically close to the people or teams you want to influence?

Deliver.

11. What can you do to exceed expectations for someone you need to get to know better?

Motivate Action

Now that you've established yourself as someone people want
to help, and you've built relationships with the people you
want to influence, it's time get people moving in the right
direction. Here's how.

Build Momentum

In physics, objects in motion stay in motion, provided they are in a frictionless environment. Businesses, volunteer organizations, and families are hardly frictionless. That said, the laws of physics still apply. Newton's First Law, sometimes called the Law of Inertia, says that objects in motion will stay in motion, and objects at rest will stay on the couch. The first step to getting things done through other people is to get them moving in the right direction.

People have a need to be consistent in their actions. Once someone takes a stance, it's hard to get them "to go back on their word," even if they have changed their mind. Knowing this is helpful when you need to get your stakeholders moving in the right direction. Rather than ask your stakeholders to help you tackle a big issue in one big step, make a request to take a small step that gets your stakeholder to demonstrate that the issue is important to them. A classic study helps to illustrate this point.

Sign if You Drive Carefully

Researchers targeted a neighborhood that had a problem with people driving too fast through the streets. They asked half of the neighborhood if they'd put a large "Drive Carefully" sign in their front lawn. Only 17% of the homeowners agreed to put this sign in their lawn.

For the other half of the neighborhood, the researchers asked homeowners to place a small, three-inch "Be A Safe Driver" sign in their window. Almost all those homeowners agreed to this smaller request. After a few weeks, the researchers went back to the homeowners who had accepted the small sign to tell them that the small sign strategy wasn't working, and asked whether they'd be willing to place a larger lawn sign in their yard. 76% then agreed to take the larger sign (Freedman & Fraser, 1966).

Fundraisers use this technique all the time. If we make a small donation to a cause, we are much more likely to continue to donate, or raise the amount we donate over time. In effect, once we donate, we're part of the team and in it together.

When we get people to take a small step in the direction we want them to go, they're much more likely to take a bigger step later.

Focus on the Positives

People have a natural bias against losing. Losing is bad, winning is good. When presented with a decision to take action, one framed as a positive "win," and one framed as a negative "loss," people will be more likely to choose the action framed as the positive win.

For example, let's consider a patient who is ill and presented with the horrific option of choosing between a surgery that will cure their condition but might result in immediate death, or doing nothing and having only a short time left to live. If the doctor presents the surgery as having a 15% failure rate, patients are more likely to forgo the surgery than they are if the surgery is presented as having an 85% success rate (Kahneman, 2011, p. 366). Rationally and mathematically the two options are equivalent, but emotionally, we see them quite differently

When you're trying to motivate action, focus on the likelihood of a positive outcome.

Narrow the Options

We love the idea of having options. Having lots of options implies lots of autonomy, the freedom to pursue whatever course is best for us.

In reality, having too many choices slows us down. We have trouble choosing among multiple options. Because we want to compare each option to another, we bog down in "analysis paralysis." We fear making the wrong choice (Schwartz, 2004).

This plays itself out in everyday life in many ways. Deciding uses up glucose in your brain, leaving you tired and depleted (Kahneman, 2011). For example, you may have experienced the mental exhaustion that comes from:

- Choosing a college, or even helping your child choose one

- Deciding among several models of televisions

- Shopping for the perfect pair of shoes

- Picking somewhere to go on vacation

- Choosing the right investments

Companies frequently receive complaints from employees that the number of fund options available in their 401k program is too limited. Studies have shown, however that participation drops by 2% for every 10 additional funds added to a plan (Heath & Heath, 2010, pp. 50-51). People choose not to participate when there are too many choices to make.

At work, we love to present lots of options, usually because we want to demonstrate how creative, diligent and thorough we've been in identifying potential solutions. Decision-makers don't want to work that hard. Choosing one option among many choices results in an "opportunity cost" associated with the options that were not selected (Schwartz, 2004). Say you were trying to get your spouse to choose a place to go on vacation. Offering up 10 choices makes them turn down nine potentially great vacations, resulting in some disappointment and a lack of enthusiasm for the vacation selected. Alternatively, picking between two or three alternatives will maximize the excitement and anticipation of the vacation.

Narrow the options down to two or three choices. With any more than three, you risk disappointment in a decision, or worse, inaction due to indecision.

Use a Good Anchor

When we decide, we compare one option to another. We always judge things in comparison to something else. Anchoring means that the first option we hear or see is our "anchor" and we judge everything else in relation to that. So it is useful for your stakeholders to have the right anchor for the action you recommend they take.

Let me emphasize that the first choice we offer will be the anchor, whether we've considered it thoughtfully or not. Therefore, we must choose carefully the option we establish as the anchor for our stakeholder. Some might see applying this influence tactic as manipulative, which it definitely can be. But like all the other tactics I've outlined, the key here is to make sure that your actions are aligned with the needs of your stakeholders, that you have their interest in mind, not yours. If we keep this in mind, we can help our stakeholders make the best decisions.

Let's say we've identified three solutions to offer to our decision-maker. Based on our analysis of the costs, benefits and risks associated with the options, the middle-priced option is the best option for our stakeholder and the one we recommend. The lowest priced option would not address all their needs and would entail a high level of risk. The highest priced option would satisfy all their needs and reduce risk even more than the middle-priced option, but depending on how our stakeholder weighs the risks, the value of that risk reduction may not warrant the additional cost.

If we present the lowest priced option first (our anchor), our stakeholder would be anchored on that low cost. They will judge anything else as more expensive, regardless of the benefits and reduced risk.

If we present the middle, recommended, option first, the lower priced option looks attractive from a price perspective, and the higher-priced option would look expensive.

If we present the higher priced option first, the middle-priced option looks less expensive, as does the least expensive option. But because our stakeholder is anchored on the lowest risk, most comprehensive high-cost project, they are more likely to make the decision to proceed with the middle-priced option.

If you're trying to motivate action with a decision-maker who is biased against spending money (as most decision-makers are), make sure they anchor in the right place. This maximizes your chances of their taking action on an option other than the least expensive option, which may only partially solve their problem and introduce unnecessary risk.

Make It Look Simple

People tend to describe an activity they like to do in big, high-level, simple steps. If you ask someone who loves to grocery shop what that's like, it might go something like this:

> *I drive to the store, browse around and see what looks good that day, and bring it home to make a fantastic dinner for my family.*

On the other hand, if you talk with someone who finds grocery shopping tedious, you'd likely get something more like this:

> *I look for a pen and paper to make a list at home, make the list, drive over to the store, park, walk into the store, grab a cart, then start going through the list as I walk up and down every aisle. I try to get everything as I pass through the aisles of the store in order, but inevitably I miss something and have to backtrack through the store. I then look for the shortest checkout line and wait. With my luck, there's a "price check" or "excessive coupon" person in front of me. I eventually pay, roll the cart out to the car, unload the groceries into the car, drive home, unload the car, and then put everything away where it belongs.*

See the difference? Simple is good, complex is bad...and tedious.

One spring break while I was in college, five friends and I were driving from Champaign, Illinois to Daytona Beach, Florida in two cars. Just over the Georgia border into Florida, one of the cars "threw a rod," which is a repair that requires nothing less than a new engine. That left six 19-year-old kids, three shirtless, trying to flag down cars out of the 6:30 a.m. steady flow of I-75 traffic headed to spring break. Of course, this was back in the day when only TVs and radios were wireless and phones were wired. Nobody was stopping. I suggested five of us hide out of sight of the highway while the fully dressed, smallest, and least threatening of us tried to flag down a car. Within minutes, two cars had pulled over to help. We made the task look simpler.

We should describe the tasks we want our stakeholders to do in simple terms. For the tasks we don't want them to do, stretch out that description in thorough detail. For instance, we might describe the expense reporting process in simple terms, but describe the process for submitting a late expense report in much more detail, outlining many more steps. This will encourage people to submit on time, which is best for everyone.

Make it THEIR Idea

When he was president, Ronald Reagan kept a plaque on his desk that said, "There is no limit to what a man can do or where he can go if he does not mind who gets the credit." Nothing spurs action like your own idea, but your willingness to suppress your own ego for the greater good can take you far.

If you're in a position of influence, and you want people to act, find a way to make the action you want them to take their own idea. This can be done in many ways. The most common is one we've all experienced: you throw an idea out to your boss, client, or spouse and they dismiss it immediately, only to resurrect the idea two weeks later as their own. Our immediate reaction is to say, "That was my idea!" Shut down your ego long enough to recognize that you have them right where you wanted them in the first place and go with it.

The other way to help your idea become their idea is to plan a conversation with the statements and questions that will drive your stakeholder to the same conclusions you have on the best action to take. Even if you don't have time to do that, simply asking them for input and admitting that you don't have all the answers brings them into process. Either way, you've created some involvement with the stakeholder. You've also generated some ownership and accomplishment on their part in the solution of the problem. That ownership will generate even more momentum around the solution.

Prepare for Objections

Another twist on the "Make It Their Idea" strategy is the process to use when preparing for and managing objections. When you present a set of options for your stakeholder, you're bound to face questions and objections about your assumptions and proposals. Before you step into those meetings, make sure you've set aside quiet time alone or brainstorming time with your team to come up with likely objections.

Once you have that list, rather than constructing elaborate comebacks to objections, which can turn the session into a debate or an argument that will require a winner and a loser (nobody likes to be a loser), prepare yourself with a list of questions that will drive your stakeholder to think through the same issues you have already considered. You want to turn those objections into a design session. Yes, you've already thought through why your answer is the best, and yes, it will take extra time to walk this person through the same forest of possibilities you've already hacked your way through. But it's worth it.

A colleague of mine told me a story about a time she felt she could get great benefit from attending an industry conference, but her boss was very much against the idea. My colleague took a shortcut by asking her boss a simple question: "What is the percentage likelihood you will approve my attendance at the conference?" Her boss answered with, "15%." Then she asked, "Why did you pick 15% and not something lower?" What that did was get her boss talking about the benefits to her and the company of her attending the conference. The boss started to talk himself into why she should attend. She effectively got her boss to think through the opportunity so it became his idea. By creating a situation where her boss needed to think of the benefits with a well-structured question, she made it closer to his idea and got buy-in to attend.

Structuring a set of questions to get your decision-makers to consider all sides of the problem is well worth your time. By the time you're finished, it's now their idea, and you've supercharged their commitment to taking the actions you want them to take.

Appeal to Identity

Identity can be a very strong motivator. People often identify themselves as a certain type of person, or identify with a particular group. Work to align what you are asking your stakeholders to do and how they think of themselves. With identity come expectations, and expectations can be a great motivator.

Students who are prepped before a standardized test to think of themselves as an elite group of students will do better than students who are told that they are disadvantaged and likely to not do well (Dweck, 2006). In a study of 157 children starting out with a musical instrument, the best single indicator for predicting long-term success was how long the students expected to play. More than IQ, math skills, income, aural sensitivity, and rhythm, the students identifying themselves as life-long musicians significantly outlasted and outperformed their peers who planned to play in school only. People tend to behave and perform consistently with the identity they have for themselves (Brooks, 2011).

During the transformation of a large information technology organization, I was leading a team responsible for driving the organization to higher levels of maturity against an industry standard for software engineering. When we started our transformation program, the people who wrote software within the organization identified themselves as "programmers." Programmers had been around since the explosion of computer science, some forty years prior. The people within the organization weren't particularly motivated by the term "programmer," and they knew being a programmer wasn't particularly differentiating in the market. They were a commodity.

We started to shape a different story for the workforce. We pointed out that mature software organizations followed detailed methodologies with engineering rigor and discipline.

Teams of experts architected systems that were integrated and worked as designed with few if any defects. We started to refer to our own programmers as "software engineers," effectively creating a new, more energizing and prestigious identity for the workforce. We pointed out to our new software engineers that working in an organization that had been certified at a high level of maturity in the industry standard model we were using would make their resumes much more attractive to other companies, that it would boost their status in the marketplace.

I should point out that, at first, leadership was not on board with this approach. One executive questioned us with, "You're going to tell everyone they are worth more in the marketplace because of this? They are going to want more money or they'll leave." Despite the concerns that this could result in the need for higher salaries or attrition, we eventually got buy-in for the software engineer approach. After all, who wants to work for someone who is purposely holding them back?

It worked. Individuals were motivated by this new identity. They saw themselves differently, and they saw how this could enhance their marketability and long-term security. It gave them something new to learn and a new status to achieve, which also fed their engagement in the transformation. The organization did go on to achieve the targets our client expected, and the new software engineers, though more marketable, became even more loyal to our organization.

Questions for Reflection: Motivate Action

Key ideas and questions to consider:

Take advantage of our need for internal consistency.

1. How can you tap into something important to someone you want to influence and tie that to the area where you need their help?

Use a good anchor.

2. What is the best place to anchor the person you're trying to influence? High or low, easy or complex, big or small?

Use the right frame.

3. When you want to motivate action, focus on the likelihood of a positive outcome. Can you think of a situation where you might want to focus on the negative outcome instead?

Narrow the options.

4. Can you think of a situation at work that is stalled because there are too many potential options for solving the problem? How can you simplify that situation by combining or excluding options into three choices?

Make it look simple.

5. Think of something you love to do and describe the process for performing it. Then think about something you dislike doing and describe that process. Do you find yourself talking about things you like doing in

simple ways? How could you apply this at work, at
home, or in the community?

Make it THEIR idea.

6.   Say you have a GREAT idea. Now it's time to go talk to
     someone you need to buy in to your idea. What
     questions could you ask that would help the person
     you need to influence come around to your idea on
     their own?

Prepare for objections.

7.   Before you step into your next meeting with a proposal
     to your boss, ask yourself "How could they push back
     on this idea?" How would you address that objection
     with a series of questions?

Appeal to identity.

8.   Think of the person you're trying to influence. How
     would they like to see themselves? How could you
     align that kind of person with the thing you want to get
     done?

Achieve Follow-Through

This chapter covers the "finishing." Once we've overcome the initial challenge of getting people moving in the right direction, we need to keep them focused and committed through the process long enough to follow through and finish.

Create a Sense of Urgency

"To achieve great things, two things are needed: a plan, and not quite enough time."

– Leonard Bernstein

Due dates. Nobody likes them. The word "deadline" itself originated in the Civil War, specifically from the horrific Andersonville, GA prisoner of war camp where Union soldiers would be shot if they crossed the "deadline," a railing inside the prison about twenty feet from the outside walls. Over time, the term came to define any line that should not be crossed. Just hearing the term instills a bit of that feeling of fear of failure, fear of letting someone else down, fear of not making it.

But few things in this world have been accomplished without a time limit. Deadlines are very rarely "natural," like the hypothetical deadline set by a meteor careening towards the earth. Deadlines are made up things, almost exclusively set by people in a position of influence. Even the "Y2K" deadline, a near-natural deadline where computer software around the world needed to be updated to understand the year 2000 as different from the year 1900, was inadvertently set by Pope Gregory when he refined the calendar originally set by Julius Caesar.

Setting a deadline is simply setting a goal. Setting an aggressive deadline, thus creating a sense of urgency, is one of the most common, and effective, tools to spur action. That's why we have so many of them. Keep in mind, though, that deadlines (and goals) need to be realistic, so be thoughtful and leave enough time to finish the task.

But what if you don't think you have the right position or authority to set a deadline? Deadlines have a very interesting characteristic that even people with no authority can exploit:

people rarely know where deadlines come from. They just seem to exist. The assumption is that someone with authority set the deadline for a good reason and, therefore, it is important. But anyone can do it. If you need people to do something for you, set a deadline!

Create Some Scarcity

People fear missing out. Grocery stores exploit this feature when they put things on sale and say "limit four per customer." This sends a message of scarcity, creating the thought that "I had better get mine before they all run out." So, we mindlessly throw four cans of the same soup into our shopping carts instead of the one or two we had intended to buy.

Another example is "Black Friday," the Friday after Thanksgiving in the U.S. and the traditional start to the holiday shopping season. Stores have taken to opening at midnight on Friday morning to spur people to shop for the latest gadget, toy or video game console. Knowing that some scarce items might sell out early in the shopping season causes many people to fight through post-Thanksgiving food coma to make sure they're first in line to snag that supposedly perfect gift.

You can sometimes create scarcity when you're trying to get people to follow through for you. Say you would like to get a group of stakeholders to review a policy document that will affect their organization. You can set a deadline, which will help people prioritize when they should do it. You can also create some scarcity by adding something like, "I'll incorporate your input and suggestions if I receive it by Friday. Otherwise, I will publish the final document with the feedback I have received by then." That creates some FOMO, a fear of missing out. By creating a hard window within which your stakeholders can provide input, you've created some scarcity. You will be more likely to get people to follow through than you would have with a deadline alone. It can pay to play "hard to get."

Create a Sense of Obligation

When you can show that you are dependent upon someone, that someone is more likely to follow through and help you out. We feel bad when we leave someone hanging, waiting on us. Recently, one of my colleagues at work once went so far as to nickname me "Bottleneck" because I was slowing the project down by not quickly reviewing designs and deliverables. That was a kick in the gut. When people are depending on us as individuals, we feel obligated to help.

Most people do what they need to do to avoid being the roadblock along a critical path. Show that you are dependent on someone else's help to get something done, and they're more likely to follow through. An example of this tactic would be saying, "Thanks for scheduling our printer repair to be done by noon. We will need it to be fixed by then to get our invoices out on time."

If you can demonstrate that you are changing your plans based on someone else's commitment, you can also create a greater sense of obligation for that person to show up. "Sure, I can reschedule a meeting so that we can meet at that time" or "Instead of my usual evening workout, I'll plan to get up early and hit the gym so I can join you at the event tonight." If your colleague knows that you had to rearrange your schedule and be inconvenienced to accommodate them, they will be much more steadfast in keeping their commitment and less likely to cancel on you.

The Red Cross has applied this idea during their blood drives. To increase the show rate of the donors signed up for a specific time slot, they call the night before to remind people of their appointment. By adding the simple phrase, "We'll count on seeing you then" to the end of their calls, they increased their show rate from 62% to 81% (Lipsitz, Kallmeyer, Ferguson, & Abas, 1989). The phrase "We'll count on you..." created a sense of obligation.

If you want to make sure you do something you've committed to, find an "accountability buddy" who will hold you to doing it. If you want to create some motivation to get out of bed and head to the gym, find a "workout buddy" who will miss you if you choose to roll over and sleep in. A sense of obligation can be a tremendous motivator.

The final example of this is a bit more subtle. When we send out a reminder that comments are due back on the draft of a document, we often send it to a long distribution list. Long distribution lists create what I call the "Wildebeest Effect," a kind of herd mentality. The thinking goes that if I don't make comments, nobody will miss me. Someone else will surely cover the points I had anyway, because there were 25 other people on that distribution list.

To get better responses, what if we take the extra time to send the email to one person at a time on the list? Just as a wildebeest on its own is more likely to pay special attention to a passing lion, receiving a personalized email directly from someone else creates an extra obligation to respond. If you think this might not matter, consider that Microsoft Outlook even has an email filtering rule built in that allows you to filter on emails sent "to me and only to me." If someone sends an email directly to me, and only to me, the probability of that email being important for me to reply to is much, much greater than one where I am only one person in a long distribution list.

Follow Up. Expect Them to Do It.

When you ask someone to do something for you and get a commitment, act like you expect them to do it. Our words often fail to convey that we expect them to follow through. We say things like, "I know you're really busy, but have you had a chance to..." or, "Will you be able to get that to me on Friday like we talked about?" Language like that provides an out. It sounds like we don't expect them to do it, or at least lets them know we think they might not do it.

Many of us suffer from "Intention Deficit Disorder." We intend to do everything we say we will, or that we suggest would be a good idea. But sometimes we forget, or we get distracted, or we just get busy and have to prioritize. To make sure our tasks stay high on someone's priority list, we need to speak and act directly, clearly, and confidently, like we expect the task to get done.

Christine Comaford-Lynch, a serial entrepreneur, was invited to a White House event for technology VIPs. During the event, she approached then-President Bill Clinton and asked him for more federal support for entrepreneurs. He asked her right then if she would put together a proposal. She said she would. A month later, he followed up and surprised her by asking where the proposal was. That's how you follow up and demonstrate you expect it to get done.

When you first ask for a commitment and get it, give a quick summary of what they've committed to and get them to nod their head. "So, you will be able to get that to me by Friday then? Great. Thanks, that will help me out a lot." (Better yet, get them to tell you what they are going to do: see the section titled "Get Them to Say It.")

Later in the week, remind them that you're counting on them to get it done by Friday. Rather than ask them a question like, "How is that report coming? Will you still be able to get that to me by Friday?" which gives them an out, say something like, "I appreciate you offering to help on that project and getting that report to me by Friday. We are counting on that."

If they don't get it to you by the end of Friday, immediately follow up and remind them that you're waiting on that deliverable, and ask them if there's anything you can do to help them get it done. Yes, this requires some follow-up on your part, but it demonstrates that you meant for them to do it.

Eliminate the Tedium

Most people despise tedious things. Filling out tax forms, compiling expense reports, and balancing check books are all examples of common things that many people find tedious. Which tasks are considered tedious differs by individual personality style, but typically we don't like to do them because they seem to take a lot of time, they're not fun or interesting, and we'd rather be doing something else. TurboTax, Expensify, and Quicken are all very successful software applications that take some of the tedium out filing taxes, tracking and reporting expenses, and balancing your checkbook.

In general, simple solutions win. Who would have predicted 30 years ago that we'd be purchasing bags of salad instead of chopping up a head of lettuce? We no longer have to worry about losing work and data on our computers because of automatic online backup. Plug-and-play devices have made installations of a new device like a mouse or monitor non-events. All these things required tedious processes in the past. The tedium has been eliminated.

When you're asking someone for help, try to do everything you can to remove the tedious parts of the task you're asking them to help with. If necessary, offer to do the tedious part for them.

Eliminate Temptation

Self-control takes energy–it is an exhaustible resource. Self-control is a function of the pre-frontal cortex within the brain. It takes conscious thought on our part to avoid tempting things, like a plate of cookies in the middle of the conference table. We might be able to resist for a while, but eventually we get tired. We break down and grab a cookie. Research has demonstrated this phenomenon many times over (Baumeister R. F., 2012).

One classic study illustrates this point very well. College student subjects were invited to participate in a study billed as an experiment about "food perception." To make sure they were good and hungry, students were asked not to eat anything for three hours prior to the study. When they entered the room, they couldn't help but notice the smell of fresh-baked chocolate chip cookies. Then researchers placed two bowls in the center of the table where they asked the subjects to sit. One of the bowls held pieces of chocolate candy and cookies, the other was a bowl full of radishes.

The researchers had built a story that they chose chocolates/cookies and radishes because they had very distinctive tastes, and that they would be in contact with the subjects the next day to talk about what they remembered about the tastes they experienced. Half of the students were asked to eat the cookies and chocolates, but no radishes. The other half were asked to eat three radishes, but to leave the cookies and chocolates alone. Being good subjects, they all followed the instructions.

They left the students in the room for a while, to make the radish eaters get a good look at and smell of the chocolates and the cookies. The second part of the experiment then began with a different set of researchers, running what the subjects thought was a separate experiment. The researchers told the subjects that the second experiment was created to test the problem-solving skills of high school students versus college students. This got the competitive juices of the college students flowing a bit.

The problems that they were given to solve required tracing a complicated geometric shape by connecting dots without retracing lines or lifting your pencil from the paper. The experimenters wanted to see how much time each group would spend trying to solve the problem, but the puzzles were unsolvable by design.

The students who got to eat the cookies, who were not subject to temptation, tried to solve the puzzle an average of 34 times over an average of 19 minutes. The tempted students, the ones who could eat radishes but had to resist the chocolates and cookies, only tried to solve the puzzle an average of 19 times and only spent nine minutes before giving up. Why? They were mentally tired from having to resist the cookies and chocolates. Self-control becomes depleted over time (Baumeister, Bratslavsky, Muraven, & Tice, 1998). Variations on this experiment have been repeated many times over with the same outcome. Temptation is tiring.

If you want to provide food for a meeting, for example, consider setting it outside of the room, thereby minimizing the temptation for those trying to abstain while still making the food available to those who would like to indulge.

The moral of the story: to keep people focused, engaged and energized, do everything you can to eliminate tempting distractions.

Get Them to Say It

People like to stay true to their word. Once we say something aloud, it's hard to go back and contradict ourselves. To make progress in a negotiation, politicians and diplomats sometimes have to come up with elaborate negotiating tactics and processes to avoid the appearance of going back on their word, to allow them to "save face."

The concept of verbalizing a commitment is woven deeply into our culture. In America, before testifying in court, a witness takes an oath to "tell the truth, the whole truth, and nothing but the truth." The President of the United states takes an oath of office defined in the U.S. Constitution: "I do solemnly swear (or affirm) that I will faithfully execute the Office of the President of the United States, and will to the best of my ability, preserve, protect and defend the Constitution of the United States." It's a swearing-in ceremony with an oath of office, not a contract signing ceremony.

By getting someone to say they are going to do a task, we stack the deck in favor of their completing the task. Structure your questions and conversations to get your stakeholders to say what they're going to do for you. End your conversations and your meetings with something like, "Just to make sure we're on the same page, what are your action items?"

More formally, a disciplined organization makes sure someone takes notes and publishes minutes, notes, and action items after every meeting. To make that process even more effective, at the end of the meeting, ask everyone to quickly summarize their action items. If they happen to forget something, the note-taker at the meeting will then "remind" them of the things they forgot. This ensures that everyone is engaged and paying attention during the meeting and noting their action items. It also gets them to say out loud what they are going to do, further increasing their likelihood of follow-through.

Help Them Visualize How They Will Do It

Visualization is a powerful technique for improving performance at any task. Top athletes, including gymnasts, divers, golfers, and pitchers, visualize themselves performing their movements prior to performing their skill. Top speakers visualize what it will be like to give their speech and how the audience will react. Actors visualize their performance before going on stage. Visualization is a form of planning and practice.

When you are speaking with a stakeholder who has agreed to help you with a task, take the conversation one step further by asking them how they plan to accomplish the task. This question helps them think through one of the most mentally taxing parts of any project, the planning process.

Let's say you ask your boss whether she thinks it would be achievable for you to be promoted later in the year. After thinking it over, she says that she thinks you are ready and she would support you. You can end the conversation there with a polite "thank you and I'm grateful for your support," or you can continue by asking, "What are all the things that need to happen to make sure that I am promoted? What things do I need to do? What do you need to do? Who else would need to buy in to my promotion, and how can we ensure that they are bought in?" By asking these questions, you are helping her visualize what needs to be done to make it work, effectively walking her through the planning process. Planning requires more intense thought and energy than any other part of a process. Help your boss through the planning process for your promotion and you're well on your way to that new title.

Visualization is one of the most powerful techniques for helping people plan and see themselves executing a plan. It is, therefore, one of the most powerful techniques for achieving follow-through on a commitment.

Questions for Reflection: Achieve Follow-Through

Key ideas and questions to consider:

Create a sense of urgency.

1. Think of someone who you are waiting on to perform a task. What reasonable deadline could you place on them to get it done? If you feel uncomfortable setting a date, why?

Create some scarcity.

2. What meaningful consequence could you put in place for the person you're trying to influence for failing to act within a certain timeframe?

Create a sense of obligation.

3. If you changed your plans to accommodate someone else, how can you tactfully let them know to make them feel more obligated to follow through for you?

Follow up. Expect them to do it.

4. Ask yourself if you really expect someone to do what you just asked them to do. If you don't, why did you bother? If you did, how can you show or tell them that you expect it to get done?

Eliminate the tedium.

5. When you ask someone to do something for you, ask yourself how they might be affected by tedium. What tedious part of the work you need them to do for you could you eliminate for them? Are you just being lazy in not taking care of that for them?

Eliminate temptation.

9. Think of a person you need to influence. What tempting activities might be more interesting or fun than the activity you need them to do? How could you eliminate that tempting activity, if only for a while, so they could get your task done?

Get them to say it.

10. What question can you add to the end of your next meeting to cement the commitment to perform the action items? Could you simply ask, "Now, tell me again what you're going to do?"

Help them visualize how they will do it.

11. When someone says they're going to do something for you, how can you help yourself to remember to ask, "So, how are you going to do that?"

Be a Leader

If you have mastered the tactics in the previous chapters, you've established yourself as a person of character, who can build relationships, motivate action, and help people follow through on those actions. People will now see you as a leader, someone who can get things done with and through other people. It might seem like you've made it.

Far from it.

Leadership and influence, properly looked after, are skills that continue to grow. The strategies outlined in this section will help you to maintain and grow the leadership stature that you've worked hard to achieve.

Walk the Talk

To achieve and maintain influence, we have to gain people's trust. One of the hardest things to do is to always practice what we preach. Frankly, when I speak on the topic of this book, during at least part of the presentation I always feel a twinge of "I wish I was doing that better" or "Ouch, I forgot about that strategy the other day." It is hard to walk the talk and be on top of all this stuff all the time, but it's important to try.

Walking the talk demonstrates our internal consistency, our integrity. If we are going to ask people to behave in a certain way, we should behave that way ourselves.

Transparency International is an organization that tracks corruption in governments around the world. They created an index that measures the amount of corruption in a country. Researchers correlated their index to unpaid parking tickets issued to diplomats from around the world between 1997 and 2002 in Washington, D.C.

Diplomats have immunity from prosecution, so while paying a parking ticket may be the right thing to do, there is no legal consequence for not paying. Diplomats from countries low on the corruption index, like Sweden, Denmark, Japan, Israel, Norway, and Canada, had almost no unpaid parking tickets. Diplomats from countries that ranked high on the corruption index, like Kuwait, Egypt, Chad, Nigeria, Sudan, Mozambique, Pakistan, Ethiopia and Syria, had very high numbers of parking tickets, sometimes even over 200 per diplomat (Fisman & Miguel, 2007). Corruption involves not following the rules. If you're a leader in a position of influence, and you don't follow the rules, can you really expect your constituency to follow you?

It's also important to step back and look at the big picture when we're facing decisions that don't have an obvious answer. Immanuel Kant, an 18th century philosopher, wrote about ethical decision-making. Before deciding on a course of action, he proposed asking, "What if everyone did it that way?" I've had conversations about this with people during change efforts: What if everyone ignored this process? What if everyone ignored this request for assistance from another team? What if everyone had that attitude? Where would we be?

We must pay attention to what we ask from others, do our best to do those same things ourselves, and acknowledge when we fall short. Nobody is perfect, but leaders have to care enough to make their best effort.

Be Comfortable with Being Uncomfortable

Ambiguity can be a frustrating, even scary, thing. Leaders face ambiguity all the time. They have to believe that careful thought and deliberate action will sort things out and result in a clear path. But we often need to wallow in ambiguity and be uncomfortable for a while, sometimes a long while, before that path becomes clear. Get comfortable with being uncomfortable.

A colleague worked on a project where the team was struggling with ambiguity. To help people deal with it and recognize they weren't alone, they came up with a phrase and a gesture: they would say, "Embrace the ambiguity," and make a pretend hug. It lightened the tension associated with the ambiguous environment, and it reminded everyone that they would eventually work through the discomfort.

Belief that you will work through the tough, ambiguous times is an important characteristic for leaders. That belief and optimism will infect others.

Adopt a Growth Mindset

> *"Recently, I was asked if I was going to fire an employee who made a mistake that cost the company $600,000. No, I replied, I just spent $600,000 training him. Why would I want somebody to hire his experience?"*

> - TJ Watson, President and Chairman of IBM

Dr. Carol Dweck, a professor at Stanford University and author of *Mindset: The New Psychology of Success,* researches how people think about their capabilities. Dr. Dweck's research found that people fall into two categories, what she calls "mindsets." People generally have either a "fixed mindset" or a "growth mindset."

Dr. Dweck's research has found that fixed mindset people believe that their abilities are hard to change and will mostly stay the same throughout their lives. Fixed mindset people believe that they might be able to improve a given capability a little, but for the most part, they believe they are wired the way they're wired, and there's no changing that. Because of this belief, they avoid challenges, figuring they won't ever improve, so they don't even try. Negative feedback is a threat, as they believe that no matter what they do, they won't be able to change much.

Growth mindset people, on the other hand, have a view that abilities can be strengthened, like muscles. They believe that practice and effort will result in better abilities, whether it's in things like remembering names, writing, managing money, controlling their emotions, or listening. With a growth mindset, you believe that you can practice anything and get much better. People with a growth mindset experiment and try new things. Sometimes they fail, but they learn and get better the next time.

Work hard to instill a growth mindset into your organization. Make it OK to fail. Create the expectation that failures will happen. Encourage people to take sensible risks to eventually improve things.

To instill a growth mindset, recognize and praise effort rather than raw talent. Rather than acknowledge, "Wow, you're a great public speaker," tell them that you admire how far they've come and how hard they worked on their presentation skills. It sounds counter-intuitive, but it pays to reward effort, even when the results aren't there. The message is that we should reward hard work and practice. Recognize that we're not born talented at everything. The more we work at something, the better we get. Every expert started out as a novice. Companies with a growth mindset create an environment of engagement, improvement, accomplishment, and achievement.

Find What's Missing

Being a critic is easy. When reviewing a document, watching a video, listening to a song, or watching a speech, it's easy to critique what's there for you to see and hear. Critics do that all the time. A great leader, though, will figure out what's missing.

A leader I once worked for was so good at this that I've named this "The Martha Principle." Before she picked up a document or presentation to review, Martha always seemed to think about what she would want to say and how she would want to tell the story. Only then would she dive in and review the document. She would take the perspective of the reader or listener and identify the feelings certain words or phrases would evoke. Inevitably, she would find new angles to make a point, along with missing content. Those reviews were invaluable in improving our communications.

Before you review someone's work, pause for a minute to think through how you would have approached the work and what you would expect to see. Make a few quick notes, and then review the document. Compare what you expected to see with what you saw, and offer those ideas to the creator of the work. This way you will get beyond the nits and easy-to-find mistakes, and your team members will appreciate and learn from the new perspectives you provide.

It's also worth pointing out that, when delivering your review of someone's work, it's best to start with some positive feedback before you dive into everything you think is missing. Without that balance, an author can feel beaten down and could choose to discount the input.

Learn from Others, and the People You Lead – Ask for Help

Leaders, especially young leaders, sometimes think that because they've been promoted, they are expected to know more than everyone who works below them in the organization. Experienced leaders recognize that their team members have great insights, deep knowledge, and valuable skills, and they tap into those attributes.

One leader I worked with was wonderful at asking questions and learning from his team. He would ask everyone in the room for their thoughts on an approach or a decision. Then he would firmly and confidently choose a course of action. Most of the time that action was aligned to the opinions of the team. Occasionally, he would contradict us, but he'd always have a great explanation: he had extracted some new piece of information from us by asking questions and learning from us, or he would bring an insight from his experience. Then he would help everyone understand how he came to his conclusion. He was learning, and he was teaching us, at the same time.

When we ask someone for help, especially someone below us in the hierarchy, we endear ourselves to the person we've asked. They feel great about themselves because they know something the boss doesn't know. They also respect the fact we admit we don't know everything and we recognize the skills and capabilities they bring to their work.

Serve the People You Lead

Great leaders look after their teams. They do what they do because they are in the habit of serving others. It's not about them, it's about others. Placing others first is, paradoxically, in the leader's best interest. It's easy to see when a leader is in it for themselves, and people will quickly stop following someone like that.

Leadership is a privilege. Nobody really *has to* follow you. They do it because they like you and it's in their best interest, and it's in their best interest because you are helping them achieve their goals.

One way to serve the people you lead is to reflect credit for your and your organization's achievements. Don't deny that you had something to do with it, but rather point out that "our team did a great job on this." Great quarterbacks, for example, will reflect credit back on the team for a great performance. It's not about them, it's about the team.

Jim Collins, in his book *Good to Great*, describes a leader with a humble heart as, "someone who looks out the window to find and applaud the true causes of success and in the mirror to find and accept responsibility for failure."

Take Responsibility for Influencing Others to Act

As a leader, you are 100% responsible for the organization that you lead. Nobody else can claim that, or carry that burden. Yet you are completely dependent upon the people within your organization. You can't be there for every decision they make, every behavior they choose. You need them to come through for you, and you are completely at their mercy. That is the paradox of leadership.

As parents, we face this same responsibility and paradox. We are completely responsible for how our kids turn out. To meet that responsibility, we have to teach them and instill in them that they are completely responsible for their own actions and behaviors.

Great leaders at any level of an organization adopt a stewardship mentality. When their piece of the organization is running well, or their part of the project is completed, but they see that another part of the organization is struggling, they don't shrug their shoulders and say, "I did my part." They cross organizational boundaries and see how they can help. They go out of their way to influence people outside of their direct hierarchies to take action for the good of the entire organization.

Failure is failure, whether it's your fault or not. Upon reflection you will usually find something you could have done (or not done) to reduce the risk of failure. Do everything you can to make the overall organization successful, whether or not it's in your job description.

Decide Based on Data and Fact, but Motivate with Emotion

As we mentioned earlier in the section "Decide Well," try to base your decisions on facts. Make sure you have facts, and not innuendo. Let's take this statement for example:

"They are always behind on this type of work."

That's interesting. How far behind? Are they always behind, or only sometimes? If sometimes, what percent of the time? People want to know that their leaders are making decisions based on facts and not opinions. How you decide defines your character.

Motivating people, however, is a different story. People aren't motivated by facts – especially financial data. They are motivated by emotion. If a top executive rallies the troops with the big goal of increasing earnings per share by 5% over last year, he'll be greeted with a lot of blank stares and yawns. But if he says we are going to produce better and more inexpensive products that will help struggling families to make ends meet, people will perk up and want to know more.

The best use of data, facts, and emotion should have an impact on the goals we set in our performance management processes. SMART (Specific, Measurable, Achievable, Relevant, Time-Bound) goals are rational and intentionally void of anything emotional. Without emotion, they are also not exciting or intrinsically rewarding. How about turning SMART into SMARTIE, adding Interesting and Exciting to the mix? Now you're talking about something that will get people jazzed and fired-up.

Rather than talk about how a project will reduce defects by 15%, talk about how the project will reduce frustrating rework and unpredictable weekend hours. Now you're talking about something that connects emotionally to your people. Stories help convey this emotion. Tell a story that illustrates the "why" behind the project that you're doing, and find ways to convey the benefits of those projects in human terms. Hardly anyone can tell you what your company's earnings per share was last quarter, but people almost always remember stories about the impact they're making on other people's lives.

Be Courageous

> *"Far better is it to dare mighty things, to win glorious triumphs, even though chequered by failure, than to take rank among those timid souls who neither enjoy much nor suffer much, because they live in the gray twilight that knows not victory nor defeat."*
>
> – Theodore Roosevelt

Do you ever feel like you're playing it safe? People usually choose one course of action over another to minimize anxiety. They take the path of least resistance. We're all a little bit scared. But it takes courage to be a leader. You have to put yourself out there and take some risk not only to be great, but just to be engaged and happy with your work.

After I was promoted to manager at Andersen Consulting, now known as Accenture, all 2,500 or so new managers from all over the world squeezed into one large ballroom at the firm's training center. We were there to celebrate and get a dose of leadership training from the executives of the firm, some of the world's most accomplished consultants.

George Shaheen, our CEO, took the stage, congratulated everyone, and then opened the floor for questions. I admired George's courage. Previous executives who opened the floor to take questions had backup executives on stage with them, people on their team who could answer a question if they didn't know the answer. George was alone.

A bold new manager stepped up to a microphone in the room and asked, "George, to what do you attribute your success?" George stopped, paused to think about his answer, and said, "Every morning I wake up and think, 'Today is the day they're going to find out.'"

What a great lesson that was! Here was a man, leading a multi-billion-dollar global consulting firm, admitting that he didn't have all the answers, that he didn't always know what he was doing, that he felt like an impostor.

Even the people at the top of the organization are figuring it out as they go. Everyone who gets a promotion has just advanced to their next level of incompetence. Successful leaders surround themselves with good people who complement their knowledge and skills, deal with ambiguity, and make decisions with integrity to the best of their ability. In other words, they are courageous.

Push your comfort zone. Take a personal risk. Chase your passion. Tread into unknown territory. Build your influence. Then lead, and have some fun.

Questions for Reflection: Be a Leader

Key ideas and questions to consider:

Walk the talk.

1.   Which of your behaviors contradict the things you say are important? What can you do to eliminate them?

Be comfortable with being uncomfortable.

2.   Do you find yourself anxious at the beginning of a new endeavor? If so, how can you reassure yourself that's a normal feeling at the beginning of everything and that once you get moving, things will come together? How can you reassure your less experienced team members?

Adopt a growth mindset.

3.   Do you praise people who fail based on reasonable risks, or do you punish them?

4.   How can you focus on and reward the effort and improvement that people make rather than focusing only on the outcome?

5.   When people do succeed, do you reward them with a "wow, you're so good at creating these reports," or do you reward and admire the effort they put in to learn how to create those amazing reports?

Find what's missing.

6.   Do you find yourself correcting grammar, spelling and wording in a document and then returning it to the sender? How can you add more value by stepping back and asking what's missing? How can you help yourself to remember to do that BEFORE you start your review

to make sure you're not biased by the author's thoughts?

7. When you're ready to provide feedback, how can you start with some positive feedback before you dive into the things that could be better?

Learn from others, and the people you lead.

8. What could you learn from one of your team members? Could you set up some time with them to have them teach you something?

Take responsibility for influencing others to act.

9. Have you missed any opportunities to help the entire organization when you could have raised an issue about another team's performance, or better yet, could you have to offered to help other teams complete their tasks for the greater good of an initiative?

Decide based on data and fact, but motivate with emotion.

10. Does your team or family come to you with issues or complaints qualified with words like "always" or "never"? Is it really always or never? How often does it happen? What's the consequence of that behavior? Should I even be bothered with this issue?

Be courageous

11. What risk do you need to take? What is holding you back? What are you afraid of, and is that feared outcome worth keeping you from being bold and doing what you are meant to do?

Getting the Most Out of
We Can't Do It Alone

The ideas in *We Can't Do It Alone* are neither new nor profound. They are, however, highly effective when you consistently apply them. Use this book as a reference, not as something you've read to sit on your shelf, never to be opened again. The book is organized to help you generate ideas and remind yourself of things you know you should do but often forget to do. It pays to keep these ideas fresh in your mind by referring to them periodically. Even as the author, I find myself failing to apply these ideas on a regular basis. But when I do pick up the book or the presentations I do about this topic to get ideas, inevitably I am more effective.

Here are some recommendations on how to use this book yourself and with other people important to your success:

With Yourself

Consider picking up the book before each of your important interactions to spur ideas on how you could be more influential. Finding just one of these tactics that would apply during that interaction could have a profound effect on the outcome.

With Your Family

Ask your spouse or significant other to read the book with you. Find ways that you can apply these techniques as a team to influence your children, friends, neighbors and community in meaningful and positive ways. As a parent, you should find most of these tactics helpful in steering your children in the right direction without having to resort to authority- and fear-based tactics, such as grounding them or taking away privileges.

With Your Colleagues at Work

Share this book with anyone who is important to your success. Your team members will benefit from these ideas and make your overall organization more effective. Whatever you do, please don't hoard this information and keep it from the people you need to influence as your "secret weapon." If you're using it that way, you're being nefarious. Share it, so they can use it, too. The cool thing about these tactics is that if you use them in an altruistic, positive way, they make you a better person. You can get things done, you are pleasant to deal with, you're a great leader...all things that we'd want everyone to be.

With Your Community

Whether it's within your neighborhood, village, faith community, state, or country, these tactics will help you stand out as a leader. These ideas and tactics are applicable to everyone, not just people who are like us.

In the community, always remember to start with the ideas at the beginning of the book. We need to be the kind of person others want to help, and we need to have a relationship with the people we want to influence. Once they get to know us, it will be much easier to get everyone on board to an agenda that will make the world a better place for all of us.

Acknowledgements

First, I want to thank Brian Betkowski, Chris Reinking, and Nigel Zelcer, the founding partners at Jabian Consulting, for creating an amazing company culture that inspired me to finally write this book.

I also want to thank the other leaders and mentors that have had a tremendous influence on me over my life and career, including Dr. Jim Kelly, Leroy Kendricks, Carl Longnecker, Jim Nowotarski, Newenka DuMont, Jim Drayer, Larry Coates, Martha Tuthill, Hines Brannan, Tom Bell, Scott McKay, and Scott Sargent.

Thanks to my friend Mike Zowine for believing in me enough to push me to get started, even introducing me to other authors.

Thanks to Bill Genthert, a fellow amateur Renaissance Man, who reviewed an early draft of the book and is always available to bounce around ideas.

Many friends and colleagues have set an example for me by being writers and coaching me, first and foremost, Bill Treasurer: your encouragement, guidance, and example have inspired me from the moment we started working together. Thanks also to authors Randy Hain, Keith Herndon, Paige Lillard, and Liam Durbin for sharing your experiences and advice on writing and publishing.

Thank you to my father, Fred Jewell, for demonstrating through your own accomplishments that I may have a genetic predisposition to be a writer and speaker.

Many more friends and colleagues helped me through the writing, reviews and publication of the book.

First, thank you to Jennifer Nourollahi for your help with the very first draft of the book and giving me my initial momentum.

Also, thank you:

To Dr. Syl Furmanek and his wife, Maxine Furmanek, for encouraging me to write this book, donating your quiet, empty house to allow me to focus long enough to write the first draft, and reviewing the early drafts of the manuscript.

To Brian Betkowski, for reading the first draft and injecting a believable amount of enthusiasm to quell my self-doubt.

To Chris Reinking, for generating some intrinsic motivation for me by pointing out how you were using things you got out of your draft review.

To Victoria Inman, for your very thorough edits and for pointing out the positive things you got out of the book.

To Anna Pinder for your insightful edits and suggestions, and for recognizing the applicability of these concepts to so many parts of life, not just business.

To Courtney Ramey, for your suggestions and positive encouragement.

To Tracy Reznik, for your cutting insights and critical comments late in the review cycle: you found so many ways to make the book better.

To Bedeke Cresci, thank you for making sure the book stayed true to its altruistic intent.

To Nicole Decraene, whose thoughtful and very thorough review made the book clearer and more aligned to a broader audience.

To Lindsey Brandon, for your time-crunched final review of the book before it was published. You found fix so many things to fix and make the book better.

Thanks to Karen Kreider for your advice, and creative ideas along the way.

To my editor, Nancy Breuer, whose deftly applied influence made my writing more approachable, conversational, and clear.

To Bailey Rogg, whose creativity and drive helped me push the book over the finish line and out into the world.

I also want to give a very special thank you to Joe Furmanek for his spot-on cover design.

For my friends and colleagues at Jabian whom I haven't already mentioned, thank you all for the inspiration you provide daily and the support and encouragement that drove me to get this thing done.

For all of you who have touched my life and influenced me, and who I (in a very uninfluential way) have failed to acknowledge, please forgive me, and thank you for your help.

Finally, to my wife, Julie, and our kids, Maddie and Max: thank you for your love, support, encouragement, and patience with my need to share every little cool thing I've recently read or discovered. You are all the best.

Bibliography

Ariely, D. (2010). *Predictably Irrational*. New York: HarperCollins.

Baumeister, R. F. (2012). *Willpower: Rediscovering the Greatest Human Strength*. New York: Penguin Group.

Baumeister, R. F., Bratslavsky, E., Muraven, M., & Tice, D. M. (1998). Ego Depletion: Is the Active Self a Limited Resource? *Journal of Personality and Social Psychology*, 74: 1252-65.

Bellman, G. M. (2001). *Getting Things Done When You Are Not In Charge*. San Francisco: Berrett-Koehler Publishers.

Brooks, D. (2011). *The Social Animal*. New York: Random House.

Carnegie, D. (1936). *How to Win Friends and Influence People*. New York, NY: Pocket Books.

Churchill, W. S. (1959). *Memoirs of the Second World War*. Boston: Houghton Mifflin.

Cialdini, R. B. (1984). *Influence: The Psychology of Persuasion*. New York, NY: William Morrow and Company, Inc.

Cohen, A. R., & Bradford, D. L. (2005). *Influence without Authority*. Hoboken: John Wiley & Sons.

Covey, S. R. (1989). *The Seven Habits of Highly Effective People*. New York: Simon and Schuster.

Dean, J. (2013). *Making Habits, Breaking Habits: Why We Do Things, Why WE Don't, and How to Make Any Change Stick.* Philadelphia: Da Copa Press.

Duhigg, C. (2012). *The Power of Habit: Why We Do What We Do in Life and Business.* New York: Random House.

Dweck, C. (2006). *Mindset: The New Psychology of Success.* New York: Random House.

Fisman, R., & Miguel, E. (2007). Corruption, Norms and Legal Enforcement: Evidence from Diplomatic Parking Tickets. *Journal of Political Economy*, 115(6): 1020-1048

Franklin, B. (n.d.). *The Autobiography of Benjamin Franklin.*

Freedman, J. L., & Fraser, S. C. (1966). Compliance without pressure: The foot-in-the-door technique. *Journal of Personality and Social Psychology*, 4(2): 195-202.

Goleman, D. (2005). *Emotional Intelligence.* New York: Bantam Books.

Haidt, J. (2006). *The Happiness Hypothesis.* New York: Basic Books.

Hatfield, E., Rapson, R. L., & Le, Y.-C. L. (2009). Emotional Contagion and Empathy. In J. Decety, & W. J. Ickes (Eds.), *The Social Neuroscience of Empathy* (Vol. 21). Cambridge, MA: MIT Press.

Heath, C., & Heath, D. (2010). *Switch: How to Change Things When Change Is Hard.* New York: Broadway Books.

House of Commons. (1941, 07 11). *Official Report.* London: UK Parliament. Retrieved from Hansard: http://hansard. millbanksystems.com/commons/1941/dec/08/prime-ministers- declaration#column_1358

Kahneman, D. (2011). *Thinking Fast and Slow.* New York: Farrar, Straus and Giroux.

Kelly, M. (1999). *The Rythm of Life.* New York: Beacon.

Kotter, J. P. (1985). *Power and Influence: Beyond Formal Authority.* New York: The Free Press.

Lipsitz, A., Kallmeyer, K., Ferguson, M., & Abas, A. (1989). Counting on blood donors; Increasing the impact of reminder calls. *Journal of Social Psychology* 19: 1057-1067

Maurer, R. (2004). *One Small Step Can Change Your Life: The Kaizen Way*. New York: Workman Publishing.

Oates, S. B. (1977). *With Malice Towards None: A Life of Abraham Lincoln*. New York: HarperCollins.

Patterson, K., Grenny, J., Maxfield, D., McMillan, R., & Switzler, A. (2008). *Influencer: The Power to Change Anything*. New York: McGraw-Hill.

Pelham, B. W., Mirenberg, M. C., & Jones, J. T. (2002). Why Susie Sells Seashells by the Seashore: Implicit Egotism and Major Life Decisions. *Journal of Personality and Social Psychology*, 82(4), 469-487.

Phillips, D. (1992). *Lincoln on Leadership: Executive Strategies for Tough Times*. New York: Warner Books.

Kotter, John P. (1985) *Power and Influence: Beyond Formal Authority*. New York: The Free Press.

Pritchett, P. (2007). *Hard Optimism*. New York: McGraw-Hill.

Remick, N. T. (1998). *West Point*. New Jersey: RPR.

Reynolds, G. (2008). *Presentation Zen*. Berkely, CA: New Riders.

Rock, D. (2009). *Your Brain at Work*. New York: HarperCollins.

Schwartz, B. (2004). *The Paradox of Choice*. 2004: HarperCollins.

Seligman, M. P. (2007). *What You Can Change and What You Can't*. NY: Vintage Books.

Tannen, D. (1992). *You Just Don't Understand: Men and Women in Conversation*. New York: HarperCollins.

Thaler, L. K., & Koval, R. (2006). *The Power of Nice: How to Conquer the Business World with Kindness*. New York: Doubleday.

Todorov, J. W. (2006). First Impressions - Making Up Your Mind After a 100-Ms Exposure to a Face. *17*(7). Retrieved from Princeton University: http://psych.princeton.edu/psychology/research/todorov/pdf

/Willis&Todorov-PsychScience.pdf.

Treasurer, B. (2003). *Right Risk: 10 Powerful Principles for Taking Giant Leaps with Your Life*. San Francisco: Barrett-Koehler Publishers.

Treasurer, B. (2008). *Courage Goes to Work: How to Build Backbones, Boost Performance and Get Results*. San Francisco: Barrett-Koehler Publishers.

Ury, W. (2007). *The Power of a Positive No*. New York: Bantam Dell.

van Baaren, R. B., Holland, R. W., Steenaert, B., & van Knippenberg, A. (2003). Mimicry for money: Behavioral consequences of imitation. *Journal of Experimental Psychology*, 39: 393-398

van Baaren, R. B., Holland, R. W., Steenaert, B., & van Knippenberg, A. (n.d.). Mimicry and Prosocial Behavior. *Psychological Science*, 15: 71-74.

Index

About the Author

Fred Jewell is a strategic advisor, executive coach, consultant author, and speaker on leadership, culture, engagement, change management, organization design and strategy.

Fred has over 25 years of consulting experience and is an Executive Director at Jabian Consulting. Prior to joining Jabian, he worked at Accenture for almost 20 years where he worked with clients across multiple industries in the U.S., Canada, Europe, and Asia. He has held leadership positions in many areas including workforce transformation, change management, quality management, and process improvement.

Fred holds a BS and an MS in General Engineering, specializing in Human Factors and Engineering Psychology from the University of Illinois at Urbana-Champaign. He is a frequent speaker, panelist, and moderator, and he has been published multiple times in the Jabian Journal (www.jabian.com) and Accenture's Outlook magazine.

Jewell lives in Sandy Springs, Georgia with his wife, Julie. To contact him about speaking or consulting to your organization, you can find him at:

LinkedIn: linkedin.com/in/fredjewell
twitter: @fredjewell